YOUR TOWNS & CITIES IN WC

BARNSLEY
AT WAR 1939–45

This book is dedicated to the men, women and children from Barnsley and the Metropolitan Borough who lost their lives during the Spanish Civil War, the second Great War 1939-45 and to the miners who died digging the coal

'Mark Green has written an important story about a turning point in the history of Barnsley, Yorkshire and Britain. Those of us who lived through it found it an unforgettable experience in a landscape and society still suffering from the depravation of war but, because of an inspired Attlee government, were able to look back at the period when the sun finally broke through, lit the land and changed everything. That generation and that time was the inspiration for the '60s when we began to see life in glorious colour instead of black and white.' – Sir Michael Parkinson

YOUR TOWNS & CITIES IN WORLD WAR TWO

BARNSLEY
AT WAR 1939–45

MARK GREEN

Pen & Sword
MILITARY
AN IMPRINT OF PEN & SWORD BOOKS LTD.
YORKSHIRE - PHILADELPHIA

First published in Great Britain in 2019 by
Pen & Sword MILITARY
An imprint of
Pen & Sword Books Limited
Yorkshire - Philadelphia

Copyright © Mark Green, 2019

ISBN 978 1 52672 1 877

The right of Mark Green to be identified as Author of this work has been asserted by him in accordance with the Copyright, Designs and Patents Act 1988.

A CIP catalogue record for this book is available from the British Library

All rights reserved. No part of this book may be reproduced or transmitted in any form or by any means, electronic or mechanical including photocopying, recording or by any information storage and retrieval system, without permission from the Publisher in writing.

Typeset by Aura Technology and Software Services, India

Printed and bound in the UK
by TJ International Ltd, Padstow, Cornwall

Pen & Sword Books Limited incorporates the imprints of Atlas, Archaeology, Aviation, Discovery, Family History, Fiction, History, Maritime, Military, Military Classics, Politics, Select, Transport, True Crime, Air World, Frontline Publishing, Leo Cooper, Remember When, Seaforth Publishing, The Praetorian Press, Wharncliffe Local History, Wharncliffe Transport, Wharncliffe True Crime and White Owl.

For a complete list of Pen & Sword titles please contact
PEN & SWORD BOOKS LIMITED
47 Church Street, Barnsley, South Yorkshire S70 2AS, United Kingdom
E-mail: enquiries@pen-and-sword.co.uk
Website: www.pen-and-sword.co.uk

Or
PEN AND SWORD BOOKS
1950 Lawrence Rd, Havertown, PA 19083, USA
E-mail: Uspen-and-sword@casematepublishers.com
Website: www.penandswordbooks.com

Contents

Chapter 1	Last Days of Peace – Barnsley gets Ready	7
Chapter 2	Hitler Invades Poland	62
Chapter 3	The Phoney War Ends	87
Chapter 4	Seeing it Through	150
	Endnotes	190
	Index	191

CHAPTER 1

Last Days of Peace – Barnsley gets Ready

Standing shoulder to shoulder, white gravestones adorn the green fields of France, each headstone positioned as sentries guarding the ground each Barnsley lad fought and died for in 1916, their blood still seeped in foreign soil.

Nine years after the Great War ended and with fitting ceremony the people of Barnsley paid tribute to their fathers, sons, sisters and daughters who made the ultimate sacrifice between 1914 and 1918. Breaking the poignant silence, a bugler sounded the *Last Post* followed by the *Reveille* before 150 floral tributes were carefully laid on the new War Memorial on Church Street.

Facing Regent Street was a new 8ft bronze figure of a British soldier in a greatcoat, standing at ease on outpost duty, a Union Jack draped over his head, patiently waiting to guard over the historic market town of Barnsley.

Ordained sunshine favoured the ceremony that autumn day, beating down on the 800 ex-servicemen who paraded proudly on Churchfield passing children holding flowers for their dead fathers and brothers. The former Governor of Gibraltar and well respected General Sir Charles Harington unveiled the memorial and, said, as the Union Jack slipped away, 'In honoured memory of the men and women of Barnsley who laid down their lives in the Great War 1914-1918, I unveil this memorial.'[1]

Quietly the military detachments, Territorial Service Battalions, the ex-servicemen, grieving families, along with the

The sombre soldier cast in Belgium stands guard over Barnsley.

many other organisations represented, dispersed in sombre mood. Throughout the Barnsley borough, similar unveilings of memorials proceeded, each movingly displayed as a lasting tribute to the fallen.

Days past, months turned into years, and Barnsley moved on, while time stood still for those brave men still at peace in France. Although history records how in the years after 1918, Europe and her countries were largely at harmony, she was also plagued by the undercurrent of an uneasy peace. It is difficult to say just how at peace Barnsley was: over two decades there were pit disasters, scores of industrial deaths amounting to the casualty rates of a small war, appalling living conditions (acknowledged by the ruling council) and, of course, hundreds of families still coming to terms with the premature removal of the town's flower of youth on the Somme.

In contrast to the violent winds of war being whipped up in Germany, optimism grew when Neville Chamberlain the much-maligned British Prime Minister famously waved a signed peace treaty and uttered the immortal words 'peace in our time'. Despite the confidence and with foresight the ARP (Air Raid Precaution) was mobilised, and in August 1938 the national Emergency Defence Act was passed and military reservists were called up. Before these events, in 1937 the ARP Act was passed by parliament which formally required local

This group photograph shows the officers and NCOs of a detachment of the Barnsley Home Guard. The photograph is taken outside the Eastgate Drill Hall in the centre of Barnsley (thank you to yorkandlancasterregimentbadges.com).

authorities to reassess their spending and provide the local population with a robust plan in the event of an aerial gas or bomb attack. Some local authorities failed to implement any organisation of ARP, the desire to minimise rates taking precedence. Barnsley Council demonstrated initial reluctance to implement the policy as a matter of principle.

Early signs of organisation in the town appeared as a weekly feature in the *Barnsley Chronicle* highlighting official suggestions for factories and business premises. This was in response to the Barnsley Chamber of Commerce who requested the paper to print extracts from the *ARP Handbook No. 6* (1st edition). No. 6 was specifically intended for businesses and occupiers of large commercial premises and would advise readers of the main sources of danger in an air raid: high explosive bombs, incendiary bombs, and gas bombs or gas spray. Machine-gun fire was also considered as a danger.

Badge of the Barnsley Co-operative ARP.

The world famous Grimethorpe Band marching through Cudworth just before the war; the band was heading towards the Parish Church.

Barnsley in 1938 was splattered with heavy industry. Most men eked out a living by working in coal mines, mills and the glass works. Folks would travel from outlying towns and villages to a bustling town centre that included the famous market which had 100 butchers who bought their meat from the new model cattle market that adjoined the public abattoir on Bunkers Hill.

Famous names to the town enticed customers: Albert Hirst and his legendary pork pies and Barnsley Chop, Butterfields department store, Jacksons on Peel Street, and a plethora of cinemas. The great age of cinema-going in Britain was the 1930s; most people went at least once and sometimes twice a week. The Globe Picture House, The Empire, The Alhambra, The Ritz and the affectionately-known Bug's Hut on Britannia Street, all entertained the masses. Cinemas dotted the wider area: Cudworth hosted the Star, Royston the ABC and Elsecar the Futurist. In wartime Britain some 25—30 million cinema tickets were sold each week. Cinemas were closed on Sundays by the council, a decision that split opinion. Lovers of light, recreation, learning and fun reverted to the Stone Age on the Sabbath, a move welcomed by the clergy.

As identified by Brian Elliott in *The Making of Barnsley*, the town's landscape was changing rapidly in the 1930s. Part of this was due to the building of the

Aerial photo of Barnsley town centre in 1938 just before the war.

Pillared structure making the centre platform of the new bus station in 1938. The platform was shaped like a ship's deck.

Town Hall and Barnsley Technical College in that decade. The land was cleared of dense terraces and courts as well as the Barnsley Old Hall, which was the former Manor House.[2] Peel Street Mill relocated to Ireland and the redevelopment and opening of Barnsley's new bus station in 1938 injected life into the town.

Wages in Barnsley had increased; earnings which were reported to the Ministry of Labour and published in the *Ministry of Labour Gazette*[3] showed an increase from the previous year. Coal miners were paid 2 shillings extra per shift – a significant rise. Coal miners were low paid compared to other industries especially considering how dangerous mining was. The average weekly miner's wage was about £2 15s, compared to the national average weekly wage in 1938 of over £3 for an adult male over 21 and just below £2 for an adult female.

Although Barnsley endured the depression of the 1920s and 30s, living standards rose significantly towards the end of the decade, helped by the introduction of affordable hire purchase. Despite relative prosperity for some, austerity beset the majority. 'Squalor, misery darkness and filth'[4] described living conditions in certain parts of the town; controversially this description was that of the Town Clerk, Mr Gilfillan, and Major J.G.E. Rideal objected. Gilfillan continued: 'among these properties are some of the worst which it has been my lot to see. Words of mine fail to describe some of the conditions. I have seen utter squalor and misery in these properties; dampness rising both from the outside and inside walls. Upon entering some of them, we were met with the foulest of odours, and how the people live in them without using their ARP respirators is more than I can understand. I know I wished I had mine with me… [In these houses] are cellar dwellings; dark, gloomy places where the sunlight hardly ever penetrates. You will find narrow staircases, dangerous alike for young an old.'[5] At the time of me writing this book, this is still living memory for some.

YORKSHIRE COAL MINING INDUSTRY

THE COLLIERY OWNERS GIVE THE YORKSHIRE PEOPLE

THE FACTS.

A REAL PACT OF MUTUAL ASSISTANCE.

THE NATION & THE COAL INDUSTRY.

Under an Agreement which became operative in August, 1936, the Government gave power to the owners to increase the price of coal in order to provide higher wages for miners and give a fair return to capital. Here is how the Yorkshire owners have used their powers

	AVERAGE	
THE PRICE OF COAL	WEEKLY EARNINGS	OWNERS' PROFITS
1938 ... 16 10½ per ton	ALL 2 19 7	1 0·05 per ton
35 ... 13 2½ ,, ,,	WORKERS 2 6 8	7 22 ,, ,,
Increase 3 7¾ ,, ,,	Increase 12 11	Increase 4 83 ,, ,,

No complaint of an unfair increase in price has been upheld by the Independent Tribunal appointed for the protection of the consumer.

A PRE-WAR COMPARISON
1913 & 1938.

INCREASE IN THE PRICE OF COAL	5 10¼ or 53 per cent.
,, ,, THE COST OF LIVING	56 per cent.
,, ,, AVERAGE EARNINGS	26 7 or 80 per cent.
,, ,, OWNERS' PROFITS	NIL

Miners' wages had always been a contentious subject, more so before privatisation when owners viewed company profits more important than the patriotic call for coal.

Major Rideal countered, 'when the reports get to the Minister of Health, he will think that the whole of Barnsley is nothing less than a muck heap. And it's not.' Rideal clearly had not visited the 'Barebones' area of the town or some of the pit cottages dotted around the borough. Two years earlier George Orwell came to Barnsley to observe social conditions, particularly the slum areas of town Gilfillan referred to. He noted:

House in Peel Street. Back to back, two up, two down and large cellar. Living-room loft square with copper and sink. The other downstairs room the same size, probably intended as parlour but used as bedroom. Upstairs rooms the same size as those below. Living-room very dark. Gas-light estimated at 4 1/2d. a day. Distance to lavatory 70 yards. Four beds in house for eight people--two old parents, two adult girls (the eldest aged twenty-seven), one young man, and three children. Parents have one bed, eldest son another, and remaining five people share the other two. Bugs very bad—"You can't keep 'em down when it's 'ot." Indescribable squalor in downstairs room and smell upstairs almost unbearable. Rent 5s. 7 1/2d., including rates.

House in Mapplewell. Two up, one down. Living-room 14 ft by 13 ft. Sink in living-room. Plaster cracking and coming off walls. No shelves in oven. Gas leaking slightly. The upstairs rooms each 10 ft by 8 ft. Four beds (for six persons, all adult), but "one bed does nowt", presumably for lack of bedclothes. Room nearest stairs has no door and stairs have no banister, so that when you step out of bed your foot hangs in vacancy and you may fall ten feet on to stones. Dry rot so bad that one can see through the floor into the room below. Bugs, but "I keeps 'em down with sheep dip". Earth road past these cottages is like a muck-heap and said to be almost impassable in winter. Stone lavatories at ends of gardens in semi-ruinous condition. Tenants have been twenty-two years in this house and are in arrears with rent, and have been paying an extra 1s. a week to pay this off. Landlord now refuses this and has served orders to quit. Rent 5s., including rates.[6]

Subsequent political and social pressure in the coming years paved the way for a major slum clearance and refurbishment of Barnsley and its neighbouring areas. Not all the houses could be classed as slums, but in the main the ruling council agreed, and plans were put in place to remedy the disease of poverty, albeit delayed by the war. A distressing statistic appeared in the local paper: Barnsley had the highest infant mortality rate in the country.

Once the debate had finished, no one could deny that the overriding qualities of the Barnsley public transcended their current living conditions. The people's

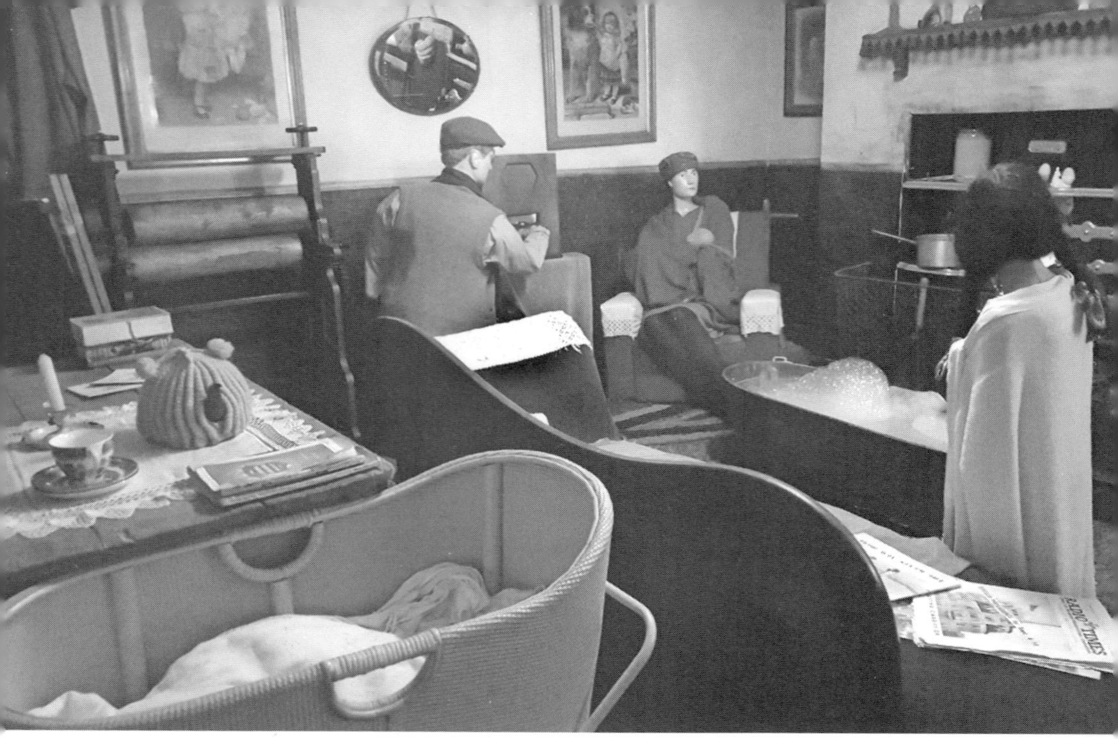

A typical working-class scene: the man is listening to the news that Britain was at war. Notice the tin bath, mangle, sparse furniture and cooking range that supplied hot water for the family. This family was lucky to have electric lighting; most houses in Barnsley at that time relied on gas mantles.

Jackson's 1938 furniture store illustrating fashions for the late 1930s family. The introduction of hire purchase made things more affordable for the masses.

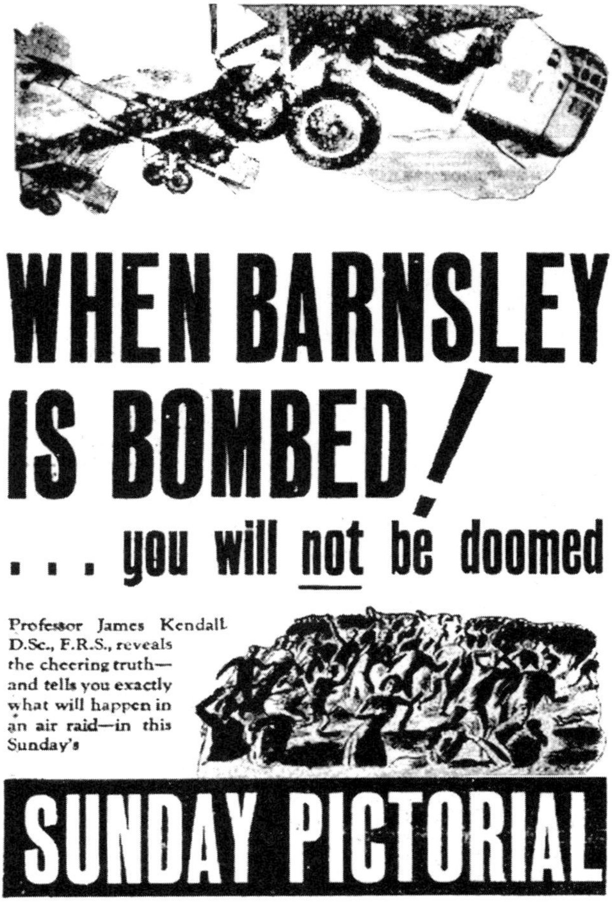

May 1938 Sunday Pictorial *getting the town ready.*

resolve was immeasurable, a community spirit and mentality whereby everyone helped each other – which would prove invaluable in the years to come.

While life in general was improving, sinister events in Europe created a sense of unease. Barnsley was not considered an immediate or high-risk target, although cities with industry would become so in time.

Barnsley and the Spanish fight for freedom

While ARP was the current buzz-word and councils focused on Report Centres, First Aid and Cleansing Posts, Decontamination Squads, Wardens, Rescue Parties, First Aid and Ambulance Services, we should also consider a small but

Flag of the International Brigade.

brave group of men from Barnsley who volunteered to defend democracy and fight fascism in Spain from 1936 to 1938.

The Spanish Civil War was a brutal conflict in which more than 500,000 people lost their lives. It was in many respects a dress rehearsal for the larger confrontation which was to envelop the world soon afterwards. Despite the British government's official policy of non-intervention, thousands of British and Irish volunteers travelled to Spain to join the International Brigades which were formed to defend the elected government of the Spanish Second Republic. The brigades were sent home in October of 1938, but not before fighting in some of the war's most critical engagements. Franco, with the support of Hitler and Mussolini, eventually led the Nationalist forces to victory and remained leader of Spain until his death in 1975.[7]

There is no shortage of disagreement amongst modern day historians whether or not the men who fought in Spain served a noble cause, but they were under no compulsion to go, and they went primarily to fight for their beliefs. William Brent (aka Forsythe), Barnsley; John Hallworth, Ward Green; Harold Horbury, Barnsley; Norman Mason (aka J. White), Barnsley; Stephen Ward, Grimethorpe; Tommy Degnan, Carlton; Bob Feasby, Clarence Wildsmith and George Henry Heppenstall of Ardsley all fought gallantly in the war, some giving the ultimate sacrifice.

Harold Horbury joined the International Brigade on 4 January 1937 and arrived in Spain three days later. Fighting not only against Spain's fascists but both Italian and German columns, Harold declared, 'I went to Spain, not because of any special love for the Spanish people but went because I love the people of all countries.' He told a packed Public Hall how he and 'Degnan [Tommy] went into action together and on the eighth day Degnan was wounded [in battle]'. Harold went into action with the 12th Battalion, which sustained 300 casualties. On their third day in the line, Tom Degnan and Bob Feasby were wounded. In July 1937 Harold was himself wounded and after a short stay in hospital was promoted to quartermaster at brigade headquarters. In August 1937, Harold took part in the first Aragon offensive, when Belchite and several other towns were captured. Later Harold was in action again at Teruel, endeavouring to stem the Fascist counter offensive. He also took part in the great Government offensive on the Ebro front.

George Henry Heppenstall, 23, joined the International Brigade at Christmas 1937. During his early service he sent letters to his home, 20 Chapel Street, Ardsley, to his mum and stepfather, Mr and Mrs Fawcett. After February 1938 his letters ceased which prompted his family to make requests to the British Red

LAST DAYS OF PEACE – BARNSLEY GETS READY

Above left: Tommy Degnan, the one-time Spanish International Brigade soldier who was working at Wharncliffe Woodmoor when the war in Spain started. After the war, 'Degs' returned to the Carlton pit and was a supporter of miners and their families for years after.

Above right: George Henry Heppenstall of Ardsley who fought with the International Brigade in Spain.

Cross and to the International Brigade for news of him. Their courage was finally recognised seventy years after the conflict when a tribute was unveiled by Mayor Margaret Morgan on 16 October 2006 with a Memorial Plaque placed in the Cooper Memorial Garden, Barnsley. It reads:

> In recognition of the contribution of the people of Barnsley to the struggle for democracy in Spain 1936-1938 and to salute the courage of those who fought against fascism in the International Brigades. They came because their open eyes could see no other way.

The front door is now the front line

Early in 1938, in readiness for the inevitable, special ARP talks had been given in Barnsley and the borough. Then in January the reconstructed Drill Hall on

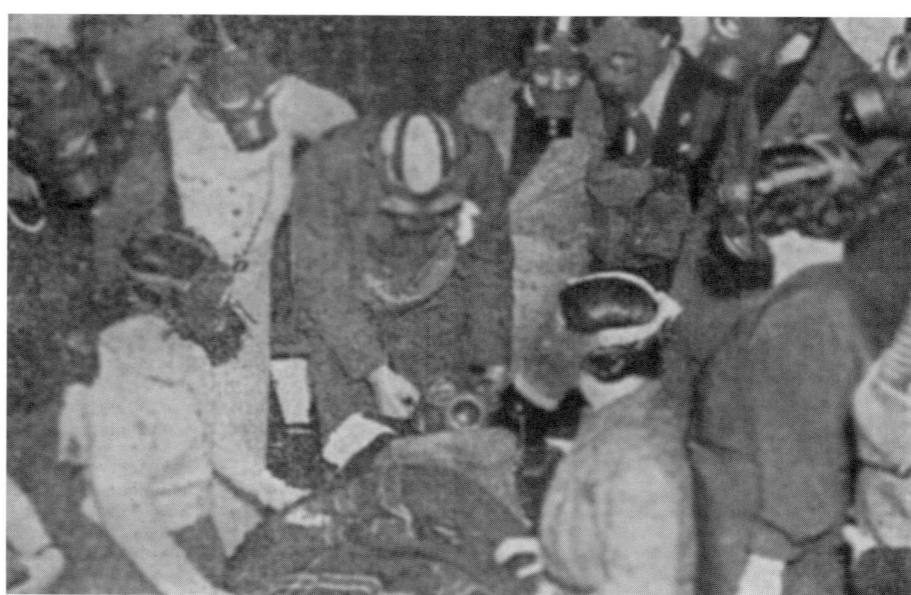

Some might have thought this was an operation on Mars in 1938: local VAD nurses receiving instruction in treating a patient affected by gas.

Eastgate witnessed the local territorials going through a gas mask drill. At the same time the Volunteer Aid Detachment nurses received instruction in treating patients affected by gas.

On the night of 8 February 1938, recommendations of the ARPs Act committee came before the council despite Alderman Raley's vacillation. The committee considered the report of the Town Clerk who chaired a meeting with the Chief Constable, the Borough Engineer, the Medical Officer of Health, Chief Sanitary Inspector and the Regional Inspector of Air Raids Precautions. With information now available the committee recommended that the Town Clerk (Gilfillan) be appointed Chief Executive Officer to coordinate the ARP services of the Corporation through the Town Clerk's department. New powers for the Town Clerk enabled him to convene meetings, issue notices to the public, organise ARP drills, and ask for volunteers for the ARP and associated concerns.

Barnsley Council, although not financially deprived, was urged by Alderman Jones to take rigorous steps to control their capital expenditure within the next few years – money would be needed for the coming war effort.

If Barnsley was at one time inclined to turn a deaf ear to the necessity of taking precautionary measures in the event of air raids, since the ARPs Act came into being, a fresh attitude was taken up; no effort was spared to make up for lost time. ARP was in vogue. Since Alderman Raley's concerns in early February the memoranda and circulars issued by the Home Office were ready to be circulated to the sub-committees, a central headquarters was identified in the basement of the Town Hall, and the Chief Constable was now able to commence classes of instruction in anti-gas training that he had communicated with the several key departments of the Corporation.

Throughout March there was a surge in administration with sub-committees established within the local urban councils.

The Assistant Clerk in Royston read communications from the Yorkshire Electric Power Company and the Royston and Brodsworth Gas Company to use Monckton Colliery buzzer as an Air Raid warning. Laughter erupted when one of the councillors pointed out that the buzzer could not be heard 'this side of the canal bridge, and if it is foggy you cannot hear it if you are standing against it.'

Tom Clayton, Hoyland ARP officer.

In Hoyland and Worsbrough Urban Council a joint plan was discussed and Tom Clayton was appointed ARP officer. Darfield sub-committee was set up in early March 1938. Dearne Valley debated their initial ARP considerations. An HQ was established at the drill hall Birdwell, and another in Penistone. In Thurlestone and Oxspring an initial review of equipment resulted in early concerns over their fire brigade equipment.

Members of the 189th AA Battery RA, TA, possibly meeting at Guest's Café on Market Hill, claiming to be the town's oldest café, established in 1765, walked slowly up to the Drill Hall on Eastgate. Instructions were communicated via a column in the local papers. These were the orders for the week ending Sunday, April 17:

Sunday, 10 April. – A Grand Band Concert in aid of Beckett Hospital, commencing at 7:45 pm admission, 6d. and 3d.
Monday, 11 April. – Section drill, gas drill and marching drill at 10 am or 7 pm
Tuesday, 12 April. – Recruit training, 10 am or 7 pm
Wednesday, 13 April. – Section drill, gas drill and marching drill at 10 am or 7 pm
Thursday, 14 April. – Recruits parade as detailed, 10 am or 7 pm

Dress for parades was overalls and caps. FS (field service) caps would have been brought to the Drill Hall and the overalls issued before parade each drill night.

Orders were similarly communicated to the Barnsley St John Ambulance Brigade (VAD) and attached nursing class. These selfless women attended the Adult School, Wellington Street.

Instructions Tuesday, 12 April: *At 6.30 pm Cadets First Aid Class. Competition test. Orderly Sergeant Cadel, Corporal Sinnett. At 7.00 pm at the Drill Hall, ARP Lecture by Divisional Surgeon T.H. Taylor.*

Steady progress was made and by 7 April 1938, 240 people had volunteered as air raid wardens and a number had enrolled as auxiliary fireman. The government had earmarked thirteen regional warehouses in various parts of the country and as soon as Barnsley was ready, gas masks would be transferred to the local depots. Major D.M.S. Mackenzie, the Regional Inspector, attended a meeting of the Technical ARP Sub-Committee at the Town Hall to assist with the preparation of the scheme. Highlights of the meeting included communication with owners of motor vehicles for assistance with emergency transportation, including the Barnsley Motor Cycle and Car Club. The Chief Constable reported that the first class of instruction in anti-gas training had been completed with his special

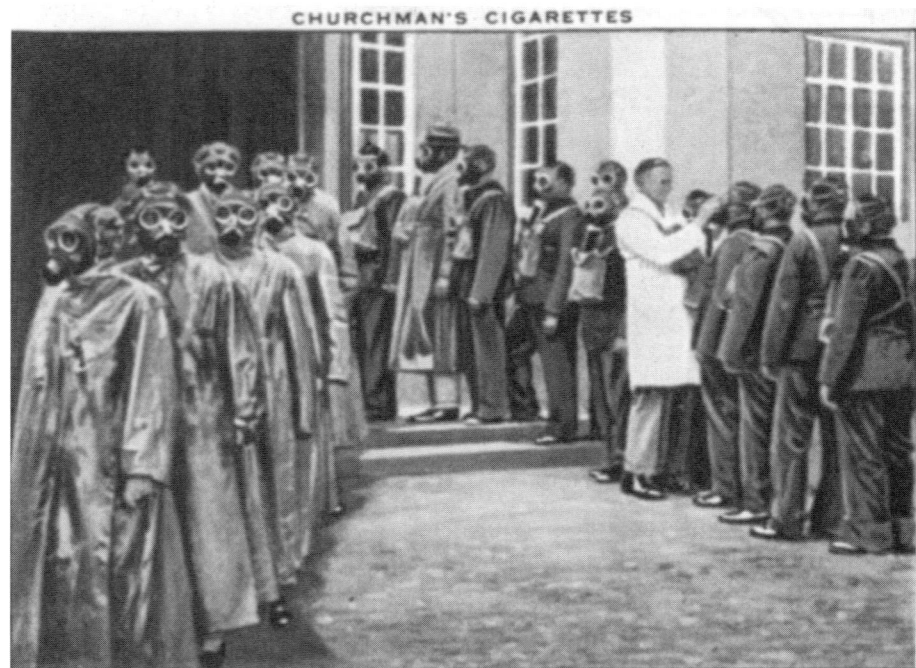

J. R. STEELE
PLUMBERS, STOVE and GRATE FITTERS, GENERAL PROPERTY REPAIRERS and CONTRACTORS.

AIR RAID SHELTERS
AT THE SHORTEST NOTICE. BUILT TO SIZE. ANYWHERE

CHURCH LANE, BARNSLEY
(opposite Beckett Hospital).
25, HOUGH LANE, WOMBWELL.

J.R. Steele diversifying his business by selling air raid shelters.

constables. Public lighting was controlled by the Borough Electrical Engineer and he was now able to manage a blackout situation as outlined by Home Office guidelines. Offers of help by Mrs England of the Barnsley VAD corps to train ARP volunteers in first aid and Dr Ball in anti-gas training were welcomed by the committee.

On the evening of 13 April, a meeting took place at the Town Hall of all the new ARP volunteers with the task of forming a rota of classes for anti-gas training.

In early May W. Humphries JP chaired a meeting of the Royston Urban Council. There was no shortage of disagreement when the ARP committee put forward suggestions to use the Wesleyan Church and the old Primitive Methodists Chapel as first-aid posts during emergency. It was further suggested that the schools on Midland Road and the Church schools be used as depots for storing civilian respirators.

A few days after the St Georges parades in Barnsley further patriotic fervour was stirred up when the 1st Battalion Yorkshire and Lancaster Regiment visited in all its pomp and glory for a demonstration tour. Showing off their weapons, work and vehicles to a packed town centre, the Mayor of Barnsley (Alderman Andrew Wright JP) took the salute from the marching soldiers.

In the week ending 7 May 1938 there were 798 service personnel recruited compared with 376 in the corresponding week the previous year. Perhaps this was due to the high-profile army demonstrations.

The Drill Hall welcomed another demonstration at the end of May when the 189th Anti-Aircraft Battery RA rolled out the 'Big Guns' in the form of the menacing AA guns. The local Terriers with instruments gauged the height and speed of aircraft above, all of which were connected and which if properly in synchronization, could target enemy planes. An interested group watched closely as the men went into action.

This demonstration was observed by a *Chronicle* reporter flying over the town from Doncaster. Gracefully the monoplane flew towards its first waypoint, the beautiful Worsbrough reservoir. Among other places the reporter distinguished the 'Town Hall, the Ritz with its brightly illuminated entrance, Harral's on Eldon Street, Barnsley Main 'muck stack', smouldering below like an angry volcano,

Cup for the Barnsley 'Terriers', the miniature rifle shooting team of the 189th Battery RA which won the Wakefield Challenge Cup in competition against all other territorial units from England. Standing (left to right) are Gunner T.E. Erwin, Lance-Bombardier J.A. Erwin, Gunner R.V. Stores and Lance-Bombardier J. Erwin. Seated: Sergeant Morley, Lieutenant J. Hall, Colonel G.S. Nelson MC, B.S.M. Barrowclough and Sergeant E. Slater.

LAST DAYS OF PEACE – BARNSLEY GETS READY 23

Above: 'Big Guns' at the Drill Hall. The Terriers practice bringing down the 'enemy' fighter over the town.

Below: Town End in 1938, exactly how the Barnsley Chronicle *reporter would have seen it as he headed towards the Drill Hall and the Barnsley Terriers.*

and Wood's Glassworks'. The roads stretched in all directions like never-ending ribbons, fighting for space with the railway lines and canals. 'Rockley Woods resembled a miniature jungle, and the countryside looked calm and peaceful with the sheep and cattle grazing in the distance.' As the aircraft banked right, the *Chronicle* man looked down the length of the gleaming wing looking for the anti-aircraft guns in the Drill Hall courtyard a mile below. The plane continued to cruise about the sky for about an hour approaching the Drill Hall from different directions before the pilot, Captain Andrew, landed back at Doncaster. Meanwhile, at the Drill Hall, the men grateful for the AA practice, stood their guns at ease.

Later the AA guns were manned, or rather 'womanned', by the ATS detachment. This was part of 2WR Company based at the regimental headquarters of 67 York and Lancaster Anti-Aircraft Regiment RA at Rotherham Drill Hall. Lady Palmer of Kirkbymoorside, or Private Edith Brewster as she was known to her colleagues, said, 'we were billeted around the town with civilians, we reported for duty at the Drill Hall early in the morning – before breakfast and left late in the evenings, after the officers had been given their evening meal.'

Members of the ATS marching past the Town Hall during a recruitment drive. (Barnsley Chronicle)

Their duties included typing, clerking, cooking and running the food stores. Edith's Barnsley tenure ended when she moved to AA Brigade Headquarters at the RAF Fighter Command station at Digby, Lincolnshire.

The demanding work and preparation continued for the Barnsley air wardens, auxiliary and full-time firemen, police and special constables when a gas chamber was opened on 24 May on Pontefract Road at the Corporations Sanitary Departments premises. Alderman Reverend D. Allott (chairman of the ARP Act Committee) declared the chamber open. Before this the volunteers had to rely on

The government gas van in Barnsley giving instruction on wearing gas masks.

the West Riding Council for use of their mobile gas van. After the opening about forty volunteers under the Act passed through the chamber, all clad in their gas masks, exposed to various concentrations of gas.

The districts too were making progress. 'Searchlights on Penistone' was the theme for the 'Great Rally' for recruits on Saturday, 28 May. The recruiting target for the day was set at seventy men, which was the required number to form a section at full strength. The 43rd (5th Duke of Wellington's Regiment) Anti-Aircraft Battalion RE Drill Hall was also officially opened by the commander of the Battalion, Colonel K. Sykes OBE MC TD JP. Beating of the drums started at 4.30 pm with the battalion band playing a selection of regimental music before beating a retreat at 6 pm. From 10.30 pm onwards, searchlights illuminated the night sky over the beautiful old market town at the foot of the Pennines.

The Battalion HQ of the 43rd was at Huddersfield and consisted of four companies, two at Huddersfield, one at Mirfield, and one distributed over the Holmfirth, Kirkburton and Penistone area. Each company consisted of four sections, each section comprising a full establishment of six searchlights. Penistone Drill Hall was a temporary one erected by the War Office to test the recruiting capabilities of the district. Each searchlight detachment consisted of ten men and was regarded by the recruiters as a splendid opportunity for a group of friends to join and form the nucleus of one of these detachments. A £5 bounty per year was paid to men who joined and attended evening training (just under two weeks wages if you happened to be a miner) in addition to the army rate of pay. The bus fare was also paid to anyone living more than 2 miles away. Later, the 43rd served in 31st (North Midland) Anti-Aircraft Brigade, protecting West Yorkshire during the Blitz. In 1940 the RE AA battalions were transferred to the Royal Artillery, and it became the 43rd (5th Duke of Wellington's) Searchlight Regiment, Royal Artillery.

Despite the inclement weather, a 'fair crowd' attended the opening of the Drill Hall. Major G.H. Oldham of the 372 Company (Holmfirth) used strong rhetoric to appeal to the men of Penistone: 'Are the men of Penistone prepared to defend their own homes, their women-folk and their children, or will they leave them to be destroyed if this district is raided from the air?'

In Hoyland and Worsbrough at the end of May, the ARP officer Tom Clayton attended a three-day intensive course on air raids at Wakefield County Hall, and an appeal for one thousand more volunteers was made in the local paper by the Town Clerk of Hoyland.

On 4 June the Coldstream Guards in full dress uniform with their distinctive scarlet tunics and bearskins paid a visit. A company billeted at Wentworth arrived at the bus depot on Upper Sheffield Road in the morning. Marching orderly the men filed from the depot along Sheffield Road, Cheapside, Queen Street and

LAST DAYS OF PEACE – BARNSLEY GETS READY

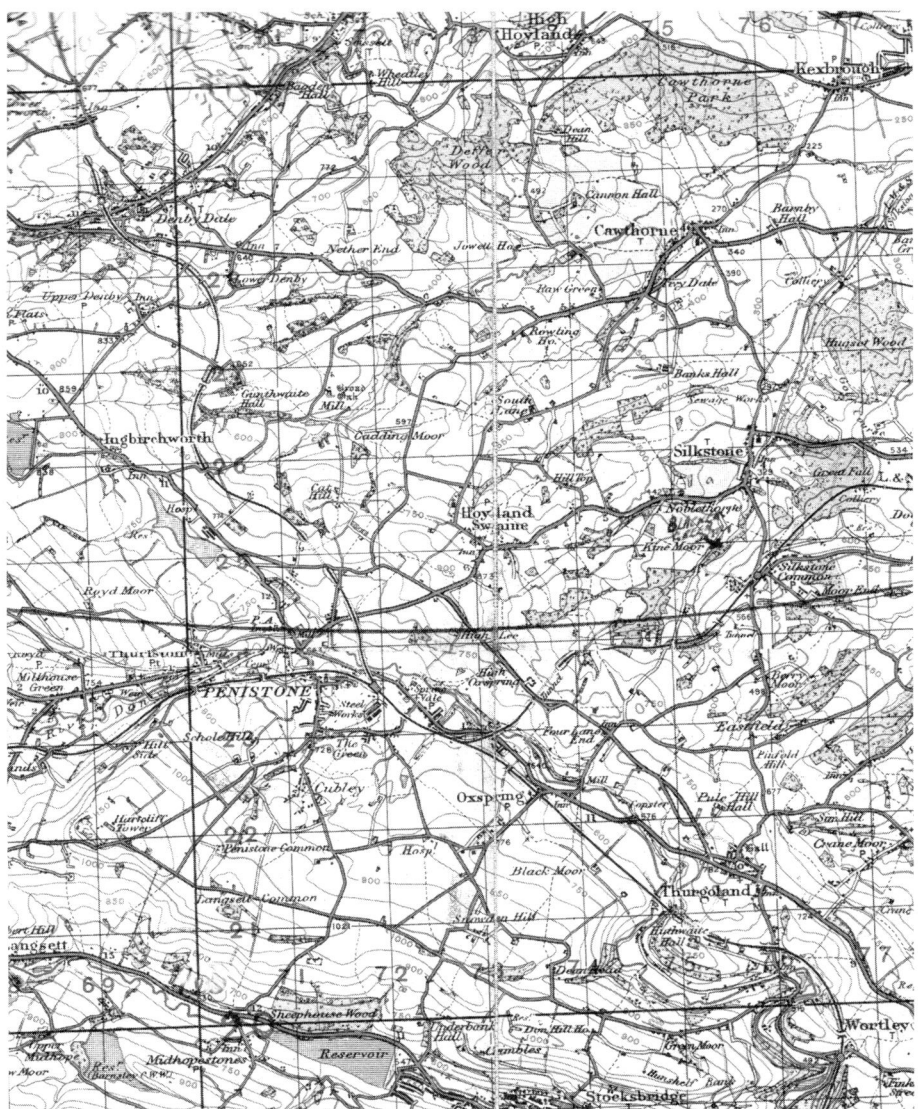

1940 Revision map of Penistone and Silkstone. (author's collection)

Market Hill to the War Memorial where a brief address was given by the mayor and a wreath was laid. Then a meal was provided in the Town Hall for the officers, and the men marched back to the depot.

Barnsley's first bomb-proof shelter was in the former wine cellar of the Old Cock Inn, Shambles Street, previously the storeroom of E. Shoesmith the

28   BARNSLEY AT WAR 1939–45

43rd (5th DUKE OF WELLINGTON'S REGIMENT) ANTI-AIRCRAFT BATTALION Royal Engineers

PENISTONE DRILL HALL
WILL BE
Officially Opened on Saturday Afternoon
MAY 28th, 1938, at 4.30 p.m.

The Battalion Band will play Selections during the afternoon in the Training Field. The Drums will beat "Retreat" at 6.0 p.m. Searchlight Equipment will be on view to the General Public. From 10.30 p.m., onwards, Searchlights will operate in and around Penistone.

THE PUBLIC ARE CORDIALLY INVITED.

RECRUITS ARE WANTED at once for the Penistone Searchlight Section. Men between the ages of **18** and **50** are invited to join and fit themselves for Home Defence.

YOUR COUNTRY CALLS
DO NOT HESITATE. ——————————— JOIN NOW.

Above: Penistone Drill Hall was a temporary building to house the Home Guard, ATS and the battery troops.

Below: Penistone Drill Hall was initially a temporary building built in May 1938 to house the local volunteers.

LAST DAYS OF PEACE – BARNSLEY GETS READY

Right and below: Alan Curtis of Cudworth in the air raid shelters at the Pontefract Road Junior and Infants school. Note the concrete sections bolted together and the blast proof iron door with WRCC (West Riding County Council) on it. (Alan Curtis, *Chewin't Cud*)

grocer (Mr Shoesmith occupied number 5 Shambles Street from 1931 to 1936). The Old Cock Inn was roughly situated where the new fountains gracefully compliment the Town Hall. The splinter- and gas-proof shelter was entered via steps from the narrow, cobbled Shambles Street. The plan was to use the shelter as a model for others to copy as local businesses were encouraged to finance and build their own shelters for staff. If called upon, this shelter could house thirty people for about two hours. Described as 'delightfully cool inside, well illuminated and spotlessly clean', the shelter boasted an air-locked door supplemented by a shutter to prevent the ingress of gas. The ARP headquarters and information bureau was in Shoesmith's old shop with the upstairs being used for demonstration and lecturing purposes. Instructors were made available to give householders practical hints on how to make their homes gas proof; gas was seen as a bigger threat than bombs at the time. Gilfillan, the chief ARP officer, used the opening as an opportunity to encourage a volunteer spirit for potential ARP helpers.

Later two large underground shelters were built in the town centre. Midland Road and Kendray Street shelters accommodated around 1,700 and the other on Barraclough's Foundry market housed 1,600.

While the June by-election was being contended in Barnsley, the Labour candidate Mr Frank Collindridge stressed the importance of peace policy

Work commencing on the first deep shelter in the market.

LAST DAYS OF PEACE – BARNSLEY GETS READY

Above and below: Views of the large underground shelter in Kendray Street, during construction and after. The photograph includes two metal containers and a curtain. Seating and electric lighting are also in place. (Memories of Barnsley)

in Europe. Other speakers attacked the government's foreign policy and advocated a return to the League of Nations that would bring real collective security. Despite pressure from the Labour Party and the fact that Collindridge won by a majority of 10,514 over his nearest rival Seymour Howard of the Liberal National party, Barnsley pressed ahead with its precautions, and provision was made by the council to stock 30,000 gas masks in three respirator stores in the town.

June was marked by healthy activity in the Worsbrough and district corps of the St John's Ambulance when all its members received training in various phases

ARP posters had been posted in most public places in and around the town.

of the brigade's work. These included an ARP instructor's course, annual VAD inspection, St Johns Ambulance Brigade inspection, gas attack displays and an interesting scenario where air raid victims couldn't get to a shelter in time.

In comparison to Barnsley, Worsbrough, Hoyland, Penistone and Royston, which seemed to be attaining a measure of success, other urban councils struggled to recruit the required number of volunteers. In Cudworth, 42 out of 120 male volunteers required had been enrolled, 21 out of 80 women and 2 out of 64 firemen – a total of 65 out of 264. Council members agreed that more should be done. They agreed to ensure that ARP volunteers and keynote speakers attended special meetings, advertisements were placed in the local press, posters were published, and Barnsley Football Club made an appeal at a football match.

Six months after the first meeting Gilfillan said to the ARP committee, 'In considering the progress made in this important duty, sight must not be lost of the fact that active steps have only been taken over a matter of months, and, having regard to the difficulties which have been encountered…it is submitted that not uncreditable progress has been made. The setting up of an entirely new organisation, both nationally and locally, is a task of immense magnitude, and it is only after years of work that an efficient system is built up.'

The numbers required and the numbers who had volunteered are outlined below:

	Personnel Required	**Volunteers**
Wardens	888	358
Auxiliary Firemen	173	50
First Aid	481	120
Other Services	332	128
Total	1,874	656

The committee had the services of four instructors qualified at the civilian Anti-Gas School. In addition, the St John Ambulance Brigade were co-operating with the committee in training people who expected to volunteer for first aid parties. Altogether 440 persons had been trained: 166 air raid wardens, 25 council workers, 39 auxiliary firemen, 130 special constables and 80 members of the police force. Gilfillan confirmed the receipt of 1,008 badges and 100 silver brooches for distribution among air raid volunteers in Barnsley. A thousand copies of the ARP handbook no. 1 had also been ordered for distribution.

It was suggested that a Barnsley blackout would be staged soon and the borough electrical engineer confirmed he had control of the lighting from one central point. One light he didn't have a button for was the burning 'muck stacks'; it was reported by Mr Griffiths, MP for the Hemsworth ARP division, that the sulphurous stacks could be seen over '200 miles away'.

Sunday, 7 August 1938, witnessed Britain's most extensive ARP experimental blackout. It was carried out from 1 to 3 am and the area covered was between the Humber and the Thames, and from Stoke-on-Trent to Cheltenham. Barnsley was amongst the centres co-operating with the RAF and elaborate preparations were made by the local ARP officers to secure darkness. To ensure the people of Barnsley assisted, Gilfillan had posters put up in public places and handbills were circulated to hotels, boarding houses and shops. Letters were sent to the big industrial concerns, factories, pits and workshops likely to be engaged on night work. The notices stressed that 'the darkening of areas exposed to air attack may be expected to be an essential feature of the defence of this country in time of war'.

Black or Bleak, two words synonymous with the town of Barnsley for hundreds of years and popularized by the writer Daniel Defoe – on a night which earlier had brought tremendous thunderclaps, vivid flashes of lightning and a freak storm turning Market Hill into a veritable cataract, at 1 am Barnsley was suddenly and completely darkened. That was apart from burning pit heaps which could not be hidden. Even the traffic signs were screened and hooded, invisible from the air. The night was described as an 'eerie experience, especially if one perchanced to be alone in the silence of those hours. Moving figures were as phantom shadows. To peep from the bedroom window, or out of doors in the sultry August night air, was almost to feel the darkness. Blackness on every hand except for a shaft of light that showed through the gloom and ghostly gleam – even that was quickly extinguished.'

The weather was so bad that no 'enemy' aircraft of the RAF were heard over Barnsley that night, but it was reported that householders observed the appeals for darkness exceptionally well. The test was a unique and strange experience to Barnsley folk, except those who had experienced the east coast in the Great War of 1914—18, for then in certain towns nearly every night meant a blackout as protection against raiding Zeppelins.

Devastating news hit the mining village of Grimethorpe when it was announced that the Ferrymore pit would have to close with the loss of 650 jobs. Alderman Andrew Wright, Mayor of Barnsley, also lost his employment at the pit. Andrew was a check weighman who monitored the recording of weights to ensure that the colliery was being honest – miners were paid by the amount of coal hewed. It made national headlines with the caption 'Barnsley Mayor on the Dole'.

The Penistone bypass was completed on 15 August 1938 at a cost of £140,000, a week before the famous Penistone Show. The district was in an excitable mood as it geared up for Barnsley Feast Week with companies advertising regular trips to the coast. Later in the war the government was to advocate 'stay at home' holidays, due to fuel restrictions.

By now nearly 40 million gas masks had been manufactured. Three types were produced: first, the 'heavy service' respirator, designed to protect wearers against continued exposure to heavy concentrations of lethal or other gases, for use by combatant services, the police force, the fire brigade, decontamination squads, ARP rescue parties and first aid parties. The second, for use by civil ARP services and persons who may have to continue normal duties in the presence of gas, was designed to give protection against everything except continuous exposure to the highest concentrations; this was called a 'civilian duty respirator'. Finally, and most common, was the 'civilian'; this was designed to protect ordinary members of the public for short periods from such gasses as phosgene, mustard gas vapour, tear gas and the so-called arsenical gases. The government issued a statement from the Home Office highlighting the testing process of the masks. Despite reassurances, some in Barnsley were not convinced of the masks' effectiveness.

A large crowd assembled on Churchfield in September to witness a 'realistic and instructive display of methods that should be used to combat the menace of bombs in the event of hostile air raiders'. Police Sergeant Hayhurst provided a running commentary of events through an amplifier. For the first time to some, a public shelter roofed with corrugated iron had been erected and incendiary bombs were lit inside. The crowd jumped as a small explosive was set off. It was then smothered with sand; this was known as the 'sand method.' Another method was the water jet.

Changes in administration for the outlying districts was confirmed in September when Tom Clayton, the incumbent ARP officer for Hoyland and Worsbrough, was appointed to the new role of ARP organiser for the area covered by the Staincross Joint ARP Committee, embracing the urban districts of Cudworth, Darton, Darfield, Dodworth, Hoyland Nether, Royston Wombwell and Worsbrough. In 1938 those eight districts had an aggregate population of 86,000 and Tom's salary was £400 per annum with travelling expenses; the average yearly salary for manual work in 1938 was £208.06.[8] Tom was a native of Pilley and joined the Sheffield 'Pals' Battalion, later transferring to the Air Force, subsequently leaving the Air Force ranked as a leading aircraftman.

A new ARP display shop opened on 22 September above the new shelter on Shambles Street. Displayed were the various respirators, clothing and implements used for protection from gas, decontamination, etc. Information was also available on ARP services and a volunteer enrolment station was established.

The national ARP recruiting drive aimed to secure 1,000,000 volunteers, and Barnsley planned to hold a special recruiting campaign during October. The district was a hive of activity to support the government in their aim.

Mayor Andrew Wright started the recruiting drive with the following heartfelt open letter:

To the townspeople of Barnsley,

You are of course, aware of the painful sequence of events which, with deep regret, we now observe have culminated in a momentous crisis affecting the lives of every man, woman and child in our beloved country.

It is my fervent hope, and one which I know is echoed in the hearts of all of you, that at this late hour reason will intervene, and peace for all the peoples concerned be secured but your council have a solemn obligation to perform, and one which they intend to fulfil with every power at their command. I refer to air-raid precaution; the protection of the civil population, the setting up of an efficient structure of precautionary measures in order to minimise to the lowest possible degree of aerial attack.

During recent days we have come to realise how urgently necessary it is that protective measures should be undertaken for the safeguarding of life and property. There is a job for every one of you. Each man or woman can play his or her part in the work of ARPs. The Council have asked me to

Children from Beech Grove School wondering what on earth these are for.

appeal to you to volunteer in one of the many services of ARPs. We ask you to do your part in the most worthy task which mankind may undertake, namely, to protect human life, property, and the homes which ever have been, and ever will be, the pride of our nation.
Andrew Wright, Mayor.

Barnsley's first consignment of gas mask parts arrived on the 27 September and were stored in the Central Depot, formerly the Falcon Engineering Works, Eastgate. Squads of volunteers were busy on Tuesday night and all day Wednesday assembling the masks so they were 'ready to wear'. The volunteers worked tirelessly to ensure the masks could be collected at the following centres:

East Ward – Grove Street Infants School and two stations at Doncaster Road Schools.
North – Two Stations at Wilthorpe Schools and two stations at Eldon Street Schools.
South – Two Stations at Racecommon Road Schools and two stations at Ellis School.
South East – Three stations at Park Road Schools and Worsbrough Common one.
South West – St George's Girls School, Pitt Street, West School and Racecommon Road Boy's School.
West – Two stations at St Mary's Boys School and Old Town Council School (Blackburn Lane).
Central – Two stations at Agnes Road Schools and two at St John's Schools.

- Monk Bretton – Two stations at Littleworth Lane (taking in Klondyke and people who polled at Miners' Welfare Hall) and Burton Road Council Schools (taking in people who polled at the Wesleyan Reform School, Carlton Road).
- Ardsley – Ardsley Oaks Council Schools, Hunningley Lane council schools, Hoyle Mill schools and Barnsley Road schools (taking in Redhill Avenue polling station).
- Darton and Woolley – Darton Hall Senior schools and Woolley Colliery schools.
- Carlton – Spring Lane Council School for the whole of the added area of Carlton.
- Birdwell - Birdwell Drill Hall on Sheffield Road.
- Cudworth – St Georges Hall and St Francis' Mission.
- Grimethorpe – The Colliery Institute.
- Wombwell – Billiard Hall, Hough Lane.
- Elsecar – The Milton Hall.
- Ryhill and Havercroft – Havercroft Junior School and Ryhill Church Hall.

Children were informed at school of the distribution places for their own streets with a brief to share that information with their household. Teachers who had ARP training worked late into the night along with many volunteers. On 29 September long queues formed, some 100 yards long. 'A' section of the 189th Anti-Aircraft Battery, Royal Artillery, TA, reported in full kit to support the gas mask distribution.

A rude awakening would have surprised some on Sunday morning if they had not been aware of a public notice issued by the Chief Constable of Barnsley, G.H. Butler. Barnsley's air raid sirens were tested for the first time. The start of an air raid would be sounded by short intermittent blasts for two minutes; then the 'all clear' would sound, a dull continuous blast of the horns for two minutes.

The following premises had the responsibility of sounding the lifesaving alarms:

- Barnsley Electricity Works, Queen's Road.
- Wood Bros. Glass Works, Hoyle Mill.
- Star Paper Mills, Old Mill Lane.
- Wharncliffe Woodmoor Colliery, Carlton.
- Qualter Hall and Co., Stocks Lane.
- Yorkshire Brick Co., Stairfoot.

'All essential services were developing well in Wombwell,' said Horace Wood, Sanitary Inspector to Wombwell Urban Council, who was directing certain aspects of ARP services. Within days of the masks arriving, 8,000 were distributed, trenches had been dug on the Hilly Fields and on Summer Lane a central first-aid post had been established in the Baths Hall, Hough Lane. Albert Barnes and Arthur Binns, Head Warden and Deputy Head Warden, appealed for volunteers to help assemble the masks and were duly rewarded with scores of women and men helpers.

The Hoyland and Worsbrough Joint ARP area had an exhibition of ARP equipment, staged at the Drill Hall, Birdwell. Police officers, ARP wardens and St John Ambulance men were on duty to answer visitors' questions.

Digging of trenches commenced at Hoyland when 200 unemployed men were set to work on two trenches, one at Platts Common and the other at Hoyland Common at the rear of Kirk Balk Senior School under the direction of Mr J.R. Shepherd, surveyor to Hoyland Urban Council. Work continued into the night with the help of flares and candles supplied by Elsecar Main Colliery.

What was believed at the time to be the first ARP decontamination centre in South Yorkshire was established in Hoyland. Tom Clayton, the ARP officer, was responsible for the general scheme, with the work directed by Decontamination Superintendent W.G. Danks, who prepared the technical details.

Guess Who? These wardens are standing in the washing room of the Hoyland decontamination centre which was the first in South Yorkshire. The man on the right was standing in the doorway of the undressing room, from which the men passed under sprays that are just visible on the top.

Housed in a building formerly used for storage in West Bank, three chambers had been constructed. In each, a stage of the decontamination process would be completed. At what was known as the decontamination end was a shed where special clothing was worn. People would then pass through the air lock and into the centre. The first chamber was the undressing room; clothes were put into galvanised iron bins. The next chamber was the washing room where sprays had been fitted for a thorough cleansing. Beyond that was a chamber fitted with lockers for civilian clothes to be stored. Just in front of that building another was constructed for the decontamination of vehicles.

At Worsbrough similar work was carried out, supervised by Mr T. Shield, surveyor to Worsbrough Council. First aid posts had also been established at the Welfare Hall, Hoyland, the Church of England Infants School, Birdwell, and the Church of England School, Worsbrough Bridge.

In Penistone, the Employment Exchange notified the district's unemployed that their services were required for digging out for bomb-proof shelters. Also in Penistone the Girl's National School and St John Baptists School were used for lectures on anti-gas methods.

Trenches in Darfield to accommodate 600 people, approximately 1 in 10 of the population, were dug at the Snape Hill recreation ground, by the side of the Mission Church, Low Valley, and the new recreation ground off County Road and Balkley Lane. Three first aid posts had been organised at Low Valley, Darfield and Millhouses.

No sooner had the gas masks been dispatched in Cudworth than the children were seen wearing theirs while riding their bikes along Barnsley Road and scaring each other in the Star cinema.

Considerable ingenuity was displayed in the provision of air raid shelters in private gardens. Some people gladly availed themselves of the Home Office's model plan for an emergency garden refuge with a corrugated iron roof and protected by sandbags. Anderson shelters were buried over a yard into the ground and covered over with a thick layer of soil and turf. Old horse boxes were also used.

Many other Barnsley *paterfamilias* got busy indoors gas-proofing a suitable room, and apparently there was a run on splinter-proof paper, special tape and gummed material for preventing the entry of gas – perhaps from Brammers of Regent Street; it was said about this newly opened shop that eventually closed in 1984, 'if you want a five legged green elephant with a glass eye, then try Brammers. If they haven't got one in stock, they'll get it for you.'[9]

Reynolds and Wadsworths, Ironmongers of Market Hill, would have experienced a brisk trade in spades, shovels and buckets. The spades, needless to state, were

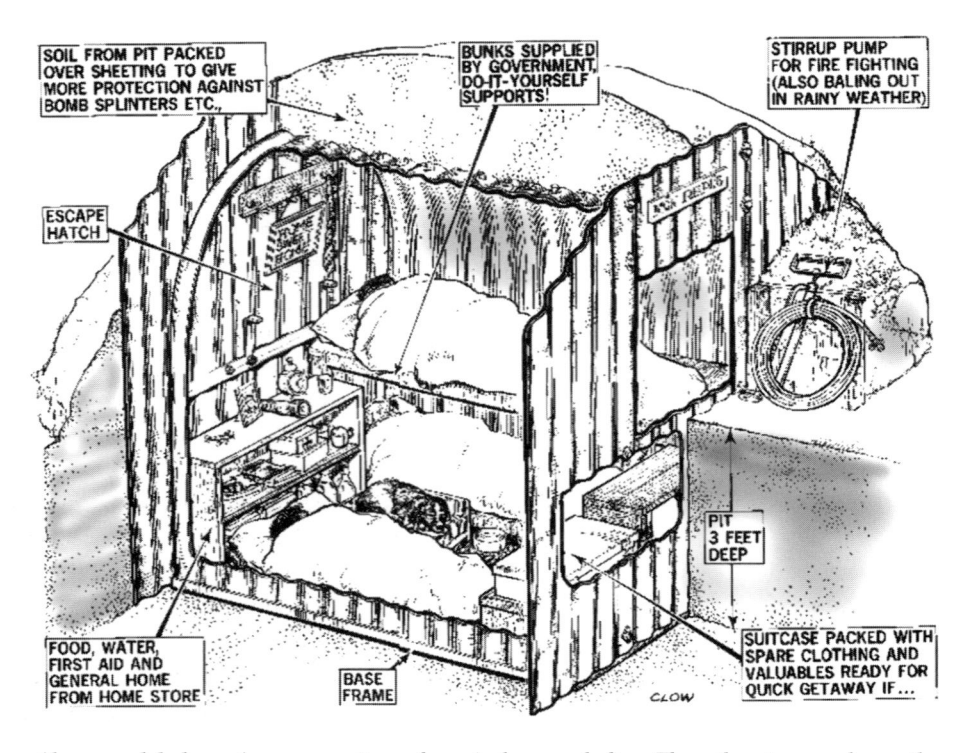

Above and below: A cross section of an Anderson shelter. The other image shows the father ushering his family into the relative safety of the shelter.

required for digging the trenches, and the demand for shovels was due to the advice to have these ready to deal with any small fire capable of extinction by dry sand or earth from buckets or boxes already filled for the emergency.

By the middle of October, 400 of the 800 ARP volunteer vacancies had been filled, meaning certain streets were left under protected. Barnsley was mapped into twenty-one areas with a head warden in charge of each, senior wardens for various streets, and a final requirement for four or five wardens for each street.

One critic of the ARP who used the *nom de plume* 'P.C. Dogberry' inferred that wardens and volunteers had not been given any instructions to help them in their role. Gilfillan, the Town Clerk, retorted with the difficulties of swift-moving events and the snags which would reveal themselves in any hastily planned event.

A person claiming to write on behalf of the people of the New Lodge Estate, Wilfred Walton of 11 Park Avenue, himself a warden, complained of the arrangements at Carlton: 'On arriving home from work at 6.00 pm my wife told me that we all had to go to Carlton School to be fitted for gas masks. We hurried and with other people caught the 6.30 pm bus to Carlton. On arrival we found a huge queue of men, women and children. Mothers stood with children in their arms until 8.00 pm and then were told there were no more masks for children. The party I was with, including women and babies, had come from the Round House Estate and were told it did not matter how far they had come and whether they had babies with them or not it was a case of first come first served. This meant that these women with their little ones had to pay bus fares again and stand once more in a long queue for two or three hours. The wardens fitted them on slowly and unhurriedly and I heard one warden grumbling they had to keep open until 10.00 pm' Joseph Shaw, an ARP warden from Carlton, took offence at this, particularly as the 'fool' had not volunteered for ARP himself. Joseph vehemently defended the organisation and the work put in by the volunteers that day.

World events unfolded with the German annexation of Czechoslovakia's northern and western border regions, formerly being part of German-Austria known as the Sudetenland at the start of October 1938. Jack boots marched on sovereign soil starting a chain reaction of events that would engulf the world in her second horrendous war of the century. Despite this, one journalist wrote in the *Chronicle*, 'the Czechoslovakian crisis…has passed and every sensible minded person hopes the peace of the world is now assured.'[10] The town was still urged to persevere with ARP plans and to assume the worst.

Players, fans and football officials at Barnsley FC lined up at Oakwell before the match with Bradford City for a short peace thanksgiving service, a similar event held throughout the football league.

This RAF recruiting van was seen at Stairfoot in 1938.

While passing through Hoyle Mill, residents heard the deep-throated roar of bombers. People looked up straining their necks to catch a glimpse. Observers would have either been confused, disappointed or amused when they looked towards Wood Brothers' glassworks and witnessed an RAF mobile recruiting office with a propaganda record playing the imaginary sound of a bomber. As the phantom bomber droned away, Sir Kingsley Wood, the Air Minister, appealed for 31,000 recruits by March 1939, before playing another recording describing all the advantages to be gained in joining the RAF. Haslam Wood, himself a keen airman, being a member of the AAF (Auxiliary Air Force) stationed at Yeadon, had invited one of the eleven vans touring the country to his glassworks at Hoyle Mill.

Another experimental blackout was planned for the night of 20 October 1938. It was suspended due to fog and restaged two days later. An ARP warden gave an account of the night:

Saturday – it was about 12:45 am as I turned off the lights, took a last look at John, my little son fast asleep, so warm, so contented, and noiselessly closing the door of his room crept downstairs and left the house. There was a 'nip' in the air as I walked to the point where it had been arranged that we should meet, about 50 of us assembled. The Chief Warden's voice, 'Fall in sections, ladies and gentlemen, section D1, D2 etc.'

A sudden darkness as every street light went out and sirens shrieked out their warning, 'hurry gentlemen,' the Chief Warden's voice again, 'answer roll.'

The roll call ended, senior wardens took over their sections. Two by two we were detailed for patrol duty. My colleague and I started our tour.

How surprised we were to see that some houses sill had lights burning, visible quite a long way off. Down across the fields we walked along the railway.

We stopped and looked up, what a clear sky. The stars twinkled, no moon – so far as the 'enemy' were concerned the conditions were ideal for an air raid.

We listened and in the distance the drone of approaching aircraft could be heard distinctly. I held my breath as I thought of my son, Felix the teddy

his pillow by his side, some marbles on his bed side chair and a book with a crayon ready for the morning. The drone of those engines coming nearer, yes my slippers were by the fire and my wife would be awake. Coats and gas masks to hand, it was only a rehearsal but she was determined to act as far as she could in case... in case...

Yes, the aircraft went over us.

My colleague and I noted the fact. We did not speak as the snorting of a railway engine somewhere down the line reminded us of life, but what of those planes above, supposing it was real....

By now bombs everywhere, I shuddered as the grim possibility forced itself upon my imagination. What of John, my wife, our home and all the other Toms and Dicks and Harrys? In my imagination I saw rows and rows of houses nothing but burning debris, destruction, horror, indescribable horror, my wife, my son, Oh God! How ghastly.

I revived my thoughts, we walked and chatted and as we passed other wardens I wondered what they had thought. What were those people thinking who had ignored the request to put out all lights? Probably nothing except perhaps we were soft to come out here.

A slight morning mist was rising as we turned and retraced out steps and made to our starting point to report our findings to the senior warden. A night-watchman on duty by some recently constructed trench shelters had put out his fire and stood rubbing his hands in the cold morning mist. Good man, he had risen to the occasion.

The Chief Warden's voice again. 'Well, ladies and gentlemen, it has been a good rally, thank you for turning out, you may dismiss, good morning.'

I hurried home as the lights flashed on again and with it my fantastic vision of the darkness disappeared. The lights of planes hurrying back to their base seemed to be dogging the twinkling skies. It had only been a 'black-out.'

I felt for my key and let myself into my house searching for the light switch, there were my slippers. I poked the fire and stirred it into a blaze. I crept into the bedroom, my wife was asleep, the gas mask was there and the coat, Johns too. I stole into his room, marbles, book and crayons were undisturbed, Felix was there as I left him. John turned in his sleep and stretched out his little hand and touched his dumb playmate on the pillow by his side.

I kissed him and said, 'it's all right old chap'. No reply but a smile of acknowledgment played upon his contented little face; 'it's all right.'

I dropped on my knees and thanked God for sparing us from what might have been and for all those men and women who had responded to the need that such an emergency would demand.'[11]

War memorials soaked in a sea of poppies were especially poignant in November of 1938, as the people of the town revived the ritual tribute to fallen soldiers. Young and old, rich and poor called to mind their kin, friends and work mates who fell in the Great War. The National Reserve Club organised the 2nd Barnsley Battalion's annual function, and members of A Company (1st Barnsley Battalion) 13th York and Lancaster Regiment met at the Ship Inn, Worsbrough Bridge.

Also, in November the opening ceremony of the reconstructed Barnsley Drill Hall, originally fixed for September of that year but postponed on account of the international crisis, finally occurred on Wednesday the 18th. A host of army dignitaries graced the occasion.

Page 10 — THE DAILY MIRROR — Monday, September 4, 1939

WANTED!

FOR MURDER... FOR KIDNAPPING... FOR THEFT AND FOR ARSON

ADOLF HITLER
ALIAS
Adolf Schicklegruber, Adolf Hittler or Hidler

Last heard of in Berlin, September 3, 1939. Aged fifty, height 5ft. 8½in., dark hair, frequently brushes one lock over left forehead. Blue eyes. Sallow complexion, stout build, weighs about 11st. 3lb. Suffering from acute monomania, with periodic fits of melancholia. Frequently bursts into tears when crossed. Harsh, guttural voice, and has a habit of raising right hand to shoulder level. **DANGEROUS!**

Can be recognized full face by habitual scowl. Rarely smiles. Talks rapidly, and when angered screams like a child.

Profile from a recent photograph. Black moustache. Jowl inclines to fatness. Wide nostrils. Deep-set, menacing eyes.

FOR MURDER Wanted for the murder of over a thousand of his fellow countrymen on the night of the Blood Bath, June 30, 1934. Wanted for the murder of countless political opponents in concentration camps. He is indicted for the murder of Jews, Germans, Austrians, Czechs, Spaniards and Poles. He is now urgently wanted for homicide against citizens of the British Empire.
Hitler is a gunman who shoots to kill. He acts first and talks afterwards. No appeals to sentiment can move him. This gangster, surrounded by armed hoodlums, is a natural killer. The reward for his apprehension, dead or alive, is the peace of mankind.

FOR KIDNAPPING Wanted for the kidnapping of Dr. Kurt Schuschnigg, late Chancellor of Austria. Wanted for the kidnapping of Pastor Niemoller, a heroic martyr who was not afraid to put God before Hitler. Wanted for the attempted kidnapping of Dr. Benes, late President of Czechoslovakia. The kidnapping tendencies of this established criminal are marked and violent. The symptoms before an attempt are threats, blackmail and ultimatums. He offers his victims the alternatives of complete surrender or timeless incarceration in the horrors of concentration camps.

FOR THEFT Wanted for the larceny of eighty millions of Czech gold in March, 1939. Wanted for the armed robbery of material resources of the Czech State. Wanted for the stealing of Memelland. Wanted for robbing mankind of peace, of humanity, and for the attempted assault on civilisation itself. This dangerous lunatic masks his raids by spurious appeals to honour, to patriotism and to duty. At the moment when his protestations of peace and friendship are at their most vehement, he is most likely to commit his smash and grab.
His tactics are known and easily recognised. But Europe has already been wrecked and plundered by the depredations of this armed thug who smashes in without scruple.

FOR ARSON Wanted as the incendiary who started the Reichstag fire on the night of February 27, 1933. This crime was the key point, and the starting signal for a series of outrages and brutalities that are unsurpassed in the records of criminal degenerates. As a direct and immediate result of this calculated act of arson, an innocent dupe, Van der Lubbe, was murdered in cold blood. But as an indirect outcome of this carefully-planned offence, Europe itself is ablaze. The fires that this man has kindled cannot be extinguished until he himself is apprehended—dead or alive!

THIS RECKLESS CRIMINAL IS WANTED—DEAD OR ALIVE!

All the above information has been obtained from official sources and has been collated by CASSANDRA

Barnsley's last Christmas at peace

Mr W. Beeson, president of the Barnsley Chamber of Trade, said it was gratifying that they had passed successfully through the national crisis and future prospects 'were rosier'. Consumers were enticed by exciting offers. J.W. Bailey of 3 Peel Street boasted a choice selection of lady's bags and purses, shopping and knitting bags, and gents' suit and attaché cases. Crossing the road to the south side, perhaps a new set of teeth from T.W. Davison's would be a better stocking filler. A trip to Millers Bargain Store on New Street would suit the austere budget. Wainwrights of Sheffield Road claimed to solve any gift problems, all assured to 'give pleasure to the recipient'. Raymond Varley of May Day Green and Whiteheads would kit anyone out for any occasion. The food from Brady Webster & Son, with numerous

Register Now For Butter-Bacon-Sugar

You will get full rationed quantity when the Government put rationing into force, and in addition at BRADY WEBSTERS you get the keenest prices for all other commodities, and personal service and attention at all our Branches.

Our travelling shops call throughout the districts, and you may register with these.

BRADY WEBSTER & SON
16, Cheapside; Town End; Sheffield Rd.; and Swift St., BARNSLEY

WOMBWELL, CUDWORTH, CLAYTON WEST, HAVERCROFT, and MAPPLEWELL.

Retailers encouraged customers to trade with them during austere times.

shops in the district, was sure to satisfy the heartiest of appetites. Or you could phone your order in to the famous Albert Hirst of Cheapside on Barnsley 2294 or 3331. Sunday, 11 December, was the big switch-on and 20,000 lamps were used to illuminate Black Barnsley.

Christmas cheer could not hide the need to press on with the ARP scheme. Captain H.A. Peter Symons, the recently appointed ARP officer for the Staincross division which included eight urban areas with a population of nearly 90,000, outlined a general scheme of work and appealed for more volunteers. In Dodworth provisions had been made for warden's classes under the supervision of Sergeant Fielding.

National Service appeared for the first time in late December when the new mayor, Councillor Cassells, received a letter from the Minister of Labour, Mr Ernest Brown, although in Parliament he had said, 'This House, recognising that the taking of measures to protect the lives and homes of the people at all times transcends in importance all party differences, welcomes the decision of His Majesty's Government to rely upon the voluntary services of the people.'

Christmas, despite the dismal weather, proved a season of good cheer in Barnsley, but 1939 did not start well for Henry and Susan Watson of Hoyle Mill Road, whose son died following a roof fall at Darfield Main Colliery on December 15. He died from cystitis due to a fractured spine a few days into the New Year.

Dodworth ARP workers being presented badges and awards from Captain Peter Symons. On the left is C. Dransfield, a keen ARP worker.

The manager of the Alhambra Cinema invited members of the ARP committee to the Walter Wanger film *Blockade* starring Henry Fonda and Madeleine Carroll. It was thought the film, about the Spanish Civil War, would have contained useful information for those engaged in ARP work. The film did encourage debate on the plight of the Spanish and more fundraising was organised.

The landlord of the Three Cranes Hotel on Queen Street, James R. Malloy, entertained a meeting of the eight constituents in the area to discuss the ARP work. Mr W. Paling, MP for the Wentworth division, expressed his appreciation for the Staincross division, comparing the confidence created to the 'panic' and 'chaos' he saw in London. Mr Frank Collindridge MP was of the opinion that the work done in Barnsley 'was outstanding' and during the crisis 'people came forward from all ranks and classes and done their bit.'

After an ARP day at the Royal Albert Hall and a radio broadcast by the Prime Minister, Barnsley's National Service Office officially opened at the end of January, the mayor opening the information bureau situated in the basement of the Town Hall. A giant thermometer that gauged the number of volunteers was erected on Market Hill encouraging people to join. By 28 January 1939 Barnsley's war strength stood at 2,600 civilian volunteers.

Above: In January 1939 the Barnsley Voluntary National Services opened in the basement of the Town Hall.

Right: National Service thermometer on Market Hill, showing there was still room for more volunteers, May 1939.

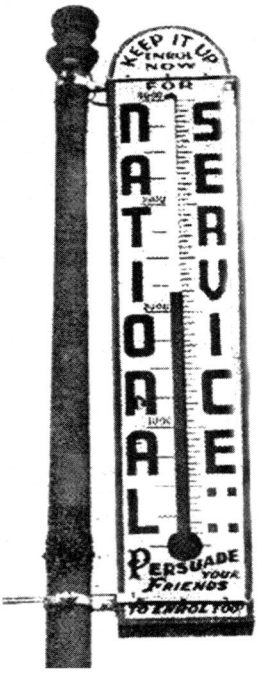

It was the end of an era in February 1939 when Mr E.G. Bayford closed his doors for the last time on his draper's shop in Eldon Street. Bayford took over the premises from John Wagstaff, himself a draper, in 1892. His father Edwin Bayford was a draper with premises at 18 Shambles Street, specialising in the 'fent' trade (cloth remnants, ends of bolts of cloth, etc). Days Radio took over the Shambles Street lease in 1899 until 1966. Bayford junior left Barnsley Grammar School in 1884 then spent time travelling the country learning his trade. Apart from his business associations, Bayford was a well-known naturalist who contributed the first general volume of the Victoria County History of York. He was also a founder member of the Barnsley Booklovers Club.

Blasting out a thunderous drone, hundreds of air raid sirens screamed in unison on a winter morning on 14 February, testing the strength and adequacy of the public warning signal. Sirens, over an area of 1,610,829 acres which housed 1,504,057 people tested the warning instruments of the West Riding area. Imagine the sound.

In the middle of February the council gave priority to all ARP work in Corporation departments and an Emergency Committee with plenary powers was appointed. Alderman Joseph Jones advised that government grants of 85 per cent would be expected for all approved ARP schemes. This was significant because since the ARP Act of the previous year there had been little central government support. The emergency committee was made up of W. Leach (chairman), Alderman J. Jones, Alderman J. Walton, Councillors A.E. McVie, H. Potter, Major J.G.E. Rideal and H. Snowden.

The committee resolved that the trenches in Huddersfield Road, Measborough Dyke and Shaw Lane be reconstructed and made permanent in accordance with the specifications issued by the Home Office at an estimated cost of £2,500; that the trenches on land in Pitt Street West and Park House Estate not to be reconstructed but left in their present condition; and the trenches on land in New Street and St Helen Hospital be filled in. They also committed to the purchase of forty trailers convertible for use as ambulances or conveyance of equipment at a total estimated cost of £1,600.

Staincross division of the ARP decided to tap into the potential resource of local women to staff first aid posts and report centres, drive cars and ambulances, to act as clerks, telephonists, despatch riders and cyclists and a certain percentage of women had to be wardens. A stirring slogan was adapted: 'It's the women we want, so join up now, ladies, and give a lead to the men.'

The same division also hit on the novel idea of producing an ARP league table with the heading, 'Look at your league table, are you satisfied or sorry' – a clear

Trenches under the ARP scheme were dug in various parts of the borough; these men prepared the trenches on Pit Street West.

attempt to prick the conscience of some and motivate others. The league tables in March stood like this:

Area	Total Volunteers required	Total Enrolled	Number required	% enrolled
Dodworth	256	180	76	70.3
Darton	490	336	154	68.5
Darfield	284	181	103	67.2
Royston	377	230	147	61.2
Hoyland	567	320	247	56.4
Cudworth	368	191	177	51.9
Worsbrough	583	295	288	50.6
Wombwell	701	313	388	44.7

As Barnsley Football Club headed the 3rd Division Football League, Dodworth headed the Staincross ARP league. A few grumblers considered the league table's subtle propaganda to be a way of scaremongering the public.

In Europe Hitler summoned President Hácha to Berlin and in the early hours of 15 March informed him of the imminent German invasion. Threatening a

Luftwaffe attack on Prague, Hitler persuaded Hácha to order the capitulation of the Czechoslovak army. Hácha suffered a heart attack during the meeting, and had to be kept awake by medical staff, inevitably giving in and accepting Hitler's surrender terms. Then on the morning of 15 March, German troops entered Bohemia and Moravia, meeting practically no resistance. Barnsley councillors expressed their condemnation of the invasion to the Prime Minister, arguing that it was a moral violation of the Munich Agreement. Councillor J. Richards recognised this further act of aggression as a game changer, announcing that Barnsley 'was in a state of emergency'.

In Barnsley, the barometer on Market Hill showed local enrolments for National Service had reached 1,448: 1,101 men and 347 women. Those were the figures announced on Friday, 7 April by Frank Hollway, secretary of the Barnsley National Service Committee.

Women especially were encouraged to call into the Exchange Buildings on Market Hill, the new office of the National Service Department or call the office on 2513 to meet the demand for 300 women drivers for ambulances and private cars. Only 42 had enrolled as of March, despite the number of women in Barnsley owning a driving license being more than 300. Mr S. Thomas, Ambulance and Transport Officer, of 4 Pitt Street, was the person charged with organising the volunteers.

ARP did much talking during the early April meeting of the Worsbrough Urban Council. There was a long discussion over an application from Mr Winter, the Chief Air Raid Warden, for the provision of an eight-inch map of the district for air raid wardens at a cost of £2 10s.

The battery orders for week ending 22 April show that the 189th AA Battery RA (TA) were taking the events in Eastern Europe very seriously. They included gun drills, Lewis gun training, air co-operation and specialist classes.

Members of Royston Council were wholeheartedly in favour of accelerating ARPs and defense measures at their monthly meeting as the consensus was that not enough was being done. Items discussed were the requirement for a morgue. The cemetery superintendent, Mr Elleker, would find a suitable place.

Mr Humphries claimed that Royston was utterly defenceless saying, 'there is not a member of this council who can point to me anything that we have done to protect our people. If an air-raid was made tonight we should all be slaughtered like sheep.' The only work done so far in Royston was the distribution of gas masks, the allocation of 23,000 sandbags and the digging of trenches paid for by the County Council. Mr Berry said that a first-aid post was required for Royston. Mr Humphries agreed and said there would be grave danger in transporting the casualties to the nearest first-aid post at Cudworth. Back then the roads between

LAST DAYS OF PEACE – BARNSLEY GETS READY 51

Barnsley 'Terriers', the 189th AA Brigade at their annual dinner.

the two townships were narrow and badly constructed making ambulance transportation difficult.

It was announced by the Air Ministry that an RAF fighter squadron was to be affiliated with Barnsley. The squadron was the 64 (Fighter) Squadron of Church Fenton. The mayor and other council members inspected a Spitfire (at this time the squadron had not officially converted to the Spitfire, that was later in 1940, although a Mk1 Spitfire was on display at Church Fenton) and the Blenheim Bombers. They were fascinated by the remarkable link trainer, a forerunner to the modern-day flight simulator. Barnsley was one of fifty-nine towns with affiliated squadrons.

On 27 April 1939, Leslie Hore-Belisha, Secretary of State for War, persuaded the cabinet of Neville Chamberlain to introduce a limited form of conscription.

A War Office Mobile Information Bureau which was in Barnsley recruiting for the Pioneer Corps.

Men called up were to be known as 'militiamen' to distinguish them from the regular army. The Act applied to males aged 20 and 21 who were to be called up for six months full-time military training and then transferred to the reserve. There was provision for conscientious objectors. It was the UK's first act of peacetime conscription and was intended to be temporary, continuing for three years unless an Order in Council declared it no longer necessary.

After an unusually hot and sunny Whitsuntide, which attracted thousands of local people to the coast, Barnsley's first registration day was Saturday, 3 June 1939. Under the regulations made by the Minister of Labour applicants were required to attend at Fenton Street off Peel Street and by Taylors Mill at strict times depending on their surname, bringing along a copy of their birth certificate. Mr Frank Hollway, manager of the employment exchange, was hoping that Barnsley's prospective militiamen would do their best to adhere to the registration timetable. After registration, examinations by a medical board, housed at the Drill Hall, would commence on 8 June from 10 am, after which the men would be allocated to their various units. Provision on a separate register was made for conscientious objectors and anyone who had a good reason to postpone their registration had to do so within fourteen days. It was reported that in almost every case they kept strictly to schedule; many were anxious not to curtail their afternoon's sporting engagements. Stanley Collins, a single miner living in Hawthorne Crescent, Dodworth, had the distinction of registering first.

Woodbine and Old Holborn cigarette smoke filled the room on Fenton Street. Many of the new militiamen commended the idea. 'It will be like a six months holiday with plenty of occupation'... 'they couldn't have chosen a better time for it'... 'now we shall be able to get sun-burnt all over'... 'perhaps we shall get time for some cricket practice, it will be worth going for it if we do.' Twenty-five years earlier Barnsley had raised two complete service battalions – the 13th and 14th (Barnsley) Battalions, the York and Lancaster, as well as a large part of the 5th and 2/5th TA battalions. The number of Barnsley militiamen enrolled in the Barnsley district on 3 June was 1,400.

A victim of its own success during the Great War, the raising of a new second line infantry battalion of the Yorks and Lancs TA was announced from the

Frank Hollway of the Employment Exchange, Barnsley.

South Yorkshire colliery districts and formed in Barnsley. The new battalion would form part of the new Territorial Field Force and be used for foreign service. Companies were raised at Wath, Dinnington and Maltby with detachments at Ecclesfield and Woodhouse. The commander would be Lieutenant Colonel Claude Errington Wales MC who was gazetted to the 3rd Battalion York and Lancaster in August 1914. Regimental Sergeant Major G.W. Pickering MM was appointed lieutenant and quartermaster. A camp was arranged for the men from 13 to 27 August near Douglas on the Isle of Man. The temporary HQ was at 1, St Mary's Gate, Barnsley, where the rent was £1 per week.

It was promised that 'foot-slogging' would be almost eliminated from the new modern army. Vickers and Lewis machine guns would be replaced by Bren light machine guns

Colonel C.E Wales, who commanded the new second line infantry battalion of the York and Lancaster Regiment, TA.

An image reminiscent of the Great War as these TAs leave for their camp at Weyburn in Norfolk in July 1939.

THE YORK & LANCASTER REGIMENT

YPRES 1915 - 1918
SOMME 1916 - 18
MESSINES 1917-18
PASSCHENDAELE
CAMBRAI 1917-18

LYS   SELLE
PIAVE
MACEDONIA
1915 - 18
GALLIPOLI 1915

SOUTH AFRICA 1899-1902

Barnsley found men for three battalions in the Great War. With the creation of a New Field Force Unit in Barnsley local youth is being given its chance. Now is the time for you to follow in your father's footsteps and join our new battalion.

ENROL NOW
at the New Recruiting Office
1, ST. MARY'S GATE
and
Stop The Dictators Dictating

DEMONSTRATION OF EQUIPMENT AT CHURCH FIELDS BARNSLEY, ON SUNDAY, JUNE 18th, from 6 p.m.

Recruitment advertising the famous York and Lancaster Regiment.

and Boyes anti-tank rifles carried by tracked Bren gun carriers and light tanks. Horses would be replaced by machines. A column of vehicles carrying samples of this new equipment departed from Sheffield and displayed their hardware on Churchfield, despite the inclement weather. A marching band headed the parade.

W.A.A.F. Recruiting Visits

VOLUNTEERS for service in the W.A.A.F. can be interviewed at:—

COOPER'S ART GALLERY, BARNSLEY,

every 2nd and 4th Thursday in the month, between 11 a.m. and 5 p.m.

WOMEN WANTED IMMEDIATELY for Administrative posts, Photographers, Clerks, Radio Operators and Radio Telephone Operators.

Barnsley had also been chosen as the recruiting centre for a unit of the Royal Army Ordnance Corps TA with the signing up of twenty-one volunteers on Monday, 12 June in a room at the Royal Hotel. This unit formed part of the

49th West Riding Division with a complement of 180 men under Captain S. Turner DFC. The age limits had been set at 18 to 54 and members would receive full army pay for men of the tradesmen classes. The Barnsley unit was one of four in the West Riding Division, covering an area from the north of Leeds to Sheffield. Birdwell Drill Hall would be used for training the new recruits.

In July the people of Barnsley witnessed a spectacular Home Defence display sponsored by the Staincross Area Panel. The grand procession included exhibits and tableaux representative of every aspect of Home Defence and an air display given at Worsbrough Bridge by Barnsley's adopted squadron, No. 64. Four of the 3-crew Blenheim Bombers of the Squadron's 'B' flight flew low, box pattern and line astern over the crowd below. Miss Gwen Watkins of Birdwell represented Britannia, symbolising the spirit of National Service. She was dressed in traditional costume, with plumed helmet and flowing flaxen hair, seated on a skilfully constructed setting featuring waves. Locke Park that day was chock-a-block with territorials, firemen and decontamination workers. 'Casualties' who had just witnessed a personal miracle, now walked sprightly with their head wounds still 'bleeding', knocking back a swift ale. Girl Guides in their trim blue uniforms, eyed up their Boy Scout 'enemies' in their green shirts and hats. Ambulance personnel and girl land workers in overalls added to the activity. Syd Walker of 'Mr Walker Wants to Know', a feature of the BBC *Bandwaggon* show, appealed to the crowd via a prerecorded speech from a loudspeaker van. Then the procession, marshalled by Superintendent H.P. Varley of the West Riding Police, left by way of Park Road and Ward Green for Dodworth, where it stopped on High Street. Here it rendezvoused with the band of the 67th Y&L AA Regiment RA TA who played and raised the spirits of the crowd, while Captain Symons of the ARP distributed leaflets on the subject of National Service recruitment. Leaving Dodworth, the procession made its way to Mapplewell via Higham Common, Barugh Green and Darton. When the parade stopped at Greenside a speech was given by Captain L. Hallam. Mr Humphries was waiting for the parade at the Wells in Royston, where hundreds of people had gathered because of their interest in National Service or at least a live band. As the procession departed for Cudworth, the sky assumed a dull hue and the heavens broke with a thunderous roar, rivalling the band for noise. Had conditions allowed, Stairfoot,

Royal Army Ordnance Corps Captain S. Turner who commanded the Barnsley contingent.

Darfield, Low Valley, Wombwell, Platts Common and Hawshaw Lane would have been visited before tea was served at Hoyland Miners' Hall. Unfortunately the rain-soaked parade could not carry on and the procession had to dry out at the Welfare Hall.

There was an unfortunate victim of the weather that Saturday when Arthur Jefferson, 46, a colliery boiler fireman of 111, Cudworth View, Grimethorpe, was thrown from a motor vehicle and died of head injuries. Arthur, a member of the Grimethorpe and the Y&L bands, was on his way back home from Cudworth when the van he was in skidded and threw him out onto the road. The coroner said, 'had it not rained, the procession would not have been abandoned at Cudworth; children would not have put their heads down and run across the road on leaving Lundwood Picture Palace; the lorry driver would not have had to brake suddenly to save the children; the bandsmen's seats would not have been wet to sit on and Arthur Jefferson would not have been thrown out onto the road.'

Weybourne on the Norfolk coast was a temporary home to miners, shop assistants, bus drivers, glass workers, clerks and others from the Barnsley district. Replacing the sulphuric air and grim looking two-up-two-downs with a stiff, fresh breeze from the North Sea blowing across two rows of white tents pitched on a slope, the men enjoyed the August sun. Bronzed men walked about shirtless, suntan accentuating their fine features.

Barnsley gunners getting into their stride by practising loading shells into one of the 3.7 guns.

Reveille sounded at 6 am. However, most days started half an hour earlier for the lads from Barnsley. Anything that shined had to be shined before their first round of physical exercise and then breakfast at 8 am. After that the men stood proud on parade, and then the chief activity of the day – training on the gun park.

Well drilled men draw up the 3.7 and 4.5-inch guns. Amongst the shell cases the miners rub shoulders with solicitors, butchers and with council officials in a bustle of preparation. Suddenly, the radio-controlled 'enemy' plane is heard, then it is seen, and hundreds of Barnsley eyes trail the target. Down on the beach the boys skilfully manoeuvre the big guns into position, loading them with shells. Waddings of cotton wool plug the ears of some of the men and as the order is acknowledged the shells pepper the sky. The entire squad stands with their mouths slightly open, almost as if they are smiling, enjoying the challenge – if your teeth are clenched when the gun triggers, the mouth bites down and the gums bleed. After an explosion, a whine and a puff of smoke one of the terriers shouts 'got it'. On the horizon another plane appears, and the men in their tin hats repeat their well-oiled routine.

Happy with their morning's work, the groups form fours. It is dinner time (not lunch for the northern men), so with shoulders back, arms swinging, boots beating out a rhythm, they march to the canteen, 1,000 men from South

The Terriers at their camp relaxing after rigorous anti-aircraft duty.

LAST DAYS OF PEACE – BARNSLEY GETS READY

Searchlight detachments worked closely with anti-aircraft guns such as the Barnsley Terriers. All were arc lamps: an electric arc was heated to 3,000 degrees and concentrated into a parallel beam by a series of reflectors. This one is on display at Eden Camp near Malton.

Yorkshire. Roast Beef, baked potatoes, greens and of course Yorkshire pudding fill the stomachs of the men. In the afternoon more training and at 5 pm the work day ends.

Some of the soldiers find relaxation on the camp's recreation ground, others spend the evening at Weybourne or at Sheringham a few miles down the coast where the hard, homely dialect of the Barnsley men mixes well with the softer vernacular of the Norfolk people.

Lance Bombardier Alf Irwin, a Barnsley bus driver, described to a reporter the miners' cooking skills in the canteen. Lance Bombardier John Caves and Bombardier Manders of 21, Newton Street, performed technical work on the potatoes, while Harold Webster, a miner at South Kirby Colliery, showed his genius as his Yorkshire puddings rose to perfection.

For some of the younger 'terriers' this was the first time under a canvas. The older men passed precious life skills down to them. Amongst the older men was Gunner George William Hitchen, of High Street, Wombwell, who was in camp at Whitby when the Great War was declared. In the summer of 1939, there was at least one father and son in the camp: Lance Bombardier Harry Cooper, of St. Helen's Street, Elsecar and his son Trumpeter Fred Cooper.

From camp life the men had the opportunity to realise their training while manning the batteries, or defence stations ringed around Sheffield. Hidden in the hills around the city the terriers swept the sky ready to fire missiles at enemy planes. These stations had been quietly gaining strength since June of '39 and all were fully operational by August, manned both day and night. The men had three types of anti-aircraft gun: the 3-inch, the 3.7-inch and the latest 4.5-inch which was capable of reaching a height of 40,000 feet. Height finders, spotters and predictors complemented the guns.

On 13 August two special trains, one leaving Sheffield and the other calling at South Yorkshire towns, took over 1,200 men and officers of the Hallamshire Battalion and the 6th Battalion Y&L to their camp on the Isle of Man, 2 miles north of Douglas at a place called Bibaloe, arriving on the SS *Tynwald* (*Tynwald* gained honour at Dunkirk saving 8,953 troops). After two weeks the troops left for Heysham by steamer.

Back home, total enrolments for National Service had reached a respectable 3,500. By mid-August 2,478 and 1,063 women had volunteered. More volunteers were still required, including seventy-four men of 'sound physique' for the Police War Reserve.

All ARP areas reported confidence with their precautions. Hoyland was assured by the chief ARP officer that all was well despite the non-delivery of promised Anderson shelters. The other areas in the Staincross division had received gas masks for babies.

After Neville Chamberlain signed the Munich agreement in 1938, he was much maligned in the press and within his own government. But it is now thought

Off to the Isle of Man. Terriers marching to the Court House on their way to their Manx camp.

that Chamberlain was playing a stalling game? It was inevitable that Hitler would break his word and Chamberlain knew it. Valuable time was bought at the expense of the relatively peaceful invasion of the Sudetenland. Barnsley, like every other town in Britain had the opportunity to prepare for war, and that time had now arrived.

Above left: Bomb 'snuffers' at the ready!

Above right: Safety for babies. A Barnsley mother demonstrating the new gas hood for babies at the Staincross ARP centre. The baby had a seat in the hood, and air was pumped in by the attachment on the right.

CHAPTER 2

Hitler Invades Poland

In contrast to the patriotic fervour that accompanied the commencement of the Great War in 1914, people in 1939 'went about their business, attending church, visiting relatives and walking in the parks.' They tuned in to their radios and listened subdued as war was announced.

In the week following the declaration of war, 600 volunteers enrolled for National Service bringing the total in the borough to 5,000, not including the boys who joined the boy scouts, ATC, Boys' Brigade and Sea and River Scouts, all of which would play their own roles in the coming years.

The Barnsley Air Cadet Corps was commanded by Squadron Leader E.H. Umbers, officer commanding the No. 148 (Barnsley and District) Squadron based at the Junior Instruction Centre, Racecommon Road. The well-appointed headquarters had a gym, parade room, officers' mess, adjutant's and squadron leader's office, secretary's office and equipment all decorated in Royal Air Force Blue.

Shops selling any kind of material to screen windows, fanlights etc. were besieged by anxious customers. Tremendous quantities of black cloth and paper had been purchased. Walter Dunk and Sons, Peel Street, had stocked up on ready-cut blackout blinds. SisalKraft blackout paper at 4½d per yard was guaranteed lightproof. Ironically some shopkeepers failed to adequately dim their own lights, prompting the efficient wardens to remind the offenders of their obligations.

David C. Bridge of Eldon Street was the first person to face prosecution when PC Banham noticed light shining through the partially closed blind of his business premises. He was ordered to pay costs and reminded of his responsibility in a blackout situation.

Badge of the No. 148 (Barnsley and District) Squadron.

Barnsley's first air raid came in the early hours of Monday, 4 September 1939. Shortly before 4 am the sirens gave the warning signal followed fifteen minutes later by the long continuous blast of the all-clear. Families would have ushered themselves into their shelters, children would have had fashioned, padded hoods to muffle the sound. It was learned the next day that the plane was in fact one of ours. Air Marshal Sir Philip Joubert de la Ferte ordered in June of 1940 that in future air raid warnings would not be sounded for a single, stray plane.

Early September was the time for children to go back to school. However, that was postponed indefinitely. A fantastic year to be a child in Barnsley!

Barnsley's first blackout victim was John Horton, a retired coal miner of 53 Shields Avenue, Worsbrough Bridge. John was knocked down by a Wakefield motorist on Vernon Road after visiting the Ship Inn, thereby providing a grim reminder of the dangers of no street lighting and the law to have car lamps dimmed. Despite warnings from the police and civil defence, three more deaths followed a few days later. Levi Cornfield (30), a colliery surface worker of Rowland Street, Royston, was knocked over near the junction of Spring Lane and Carlton Road. James Duffy (61), a railway labourer of High Street, Monk Bretton, was knocked down by a bus outside the Pheasant Inn. Yorkshire Traction

Above left and right*: Lights out. The blackout began on 1 September 1939. Speed restrictions were enforced and white lines were painted on the roads, trees and lamp posts. Although trains kept running they were slow and crowded, their carriages lit only by dim pinpoints of light.*

64   BARNSLEY AT WAR 1939–45

claimed its third victim when Garry Mitchell (49) of Barnsley Road, Stairfoot, was knocked over near the Black Bull Hotel. Scores of blackout deaths, many of them children, continued throughout the war. Pedestrians tripped over 'corsy edges', twisted ankles and crashed into each other on pavements.

Various buildings were sandbagged, including the Town Hall. The enormity of the task was illustrated when it was reported that Beckett Hospital would use 20,000 sandbags and 500 tons of sand.

One of the busiest departments in the Town Hall was the motor licensing office, with drivers eagerly snapping up petrol ration books. The mileage basis for the petrol ration was about 200 miles per month, annoying most businessmen. It was an offence to hoard petrol: four hoarders had been summoned and fined before the month ended. Electricity would also be rationed from 1 September; a pamphlet giving hints on how to use electricity more economically was produced. Gas, coal and coke was to be rationed from early October.

Petrol was a prime commodity on Barnsley's black market. In one court report four charges had been brought in a single day of either supplying or receiving petrol. 'You have both been placed in positions of trust… We shall be bound to commit you to prison and we shall have to sentence you.' Those were the remarks of the chairman of the County Borough Police Court addressed to Frank Rushforth, 49, of Racecommon Road, and Percy Coverdale Trueman

The Mayor and Mayoress at Beckett Hospital. (Barnsley Chronicle)

of 7 Kay's Terrace, Stairfoot. They were charged with stealing four gallons of petrol from the War Emergency Committee's depot in Queen's Road. Making matters worse, both were members of the ARP Rescue Squad with access to lorries and the yard. When trying to make a delivery, an eagle-eyed copper spotted them on May Day Green. Further enquiries led the constable to the Wire Trellis Hotel, the snug of the Gas Nook pub being the hub of operations. Both men were fined and imprisoned for stealing and sabotaging the war effort. Also that day, Elsie Longley of Waddington Road, John Barley of Granville Street, and Julia Carr of the Wire Trellis Hotel were all charged with receiving stolen petrol.

The 'clippity clop' of horses on Barnsley roads was a consequence of petrol rationing.

The nerve centre for ARP operations was in the basement of the Town Hall. All the Town Hall staff were expected to be involved in air raid preparations of some sort. Ladies were to operate the telephones in the newly refurbished and reinforced Civil Defence control room. They could immediately contact any of the patrol stations, first aid posts, fire stations or the auxiliary fire service, decontamination depots and squads, ambulances, repair services, or light or heavy rescue parties.

A view of the Barnsley ARP control room in the basement of the Town Hall.

Eileen Umpleby worked in the Town Hall from the outbreak of the war: 'The control room was rectangular in shape, a large-scale map of the borough occupying one long wall, covered by curtains when not in use. On the opposite wall was a row of telephone booths where we sat during a raid, awaiting calls... The warnings of approaching enemy air-craft were classed as yellow, purple or red, in that sequence of danger. The sirens were sounded for the whole town to take shelter on a red alert.'[12]

A bombing scenario was described to a visitor: 'Phone rings. Call from air raid warden's post. Text of message runs "Barnsley Chronicle office hit by H.E. bomb, twenty workmen casualties, under wreckage, no fire. Water main and gas main damaged. Eastgate is blocked." Then is given time of occurrences. The message, written in triplicate, is immediately brought to the tables at which are seated representatives of the various departments. Messages are at once dispatched over the phone for ambulances and first aid parties to proceed to the spot, the officer of the Highways Department quickly makes up his mind whether a light or heavy rescue party is required.'

There were two large scale maps of the County Borough hanging on the walls, one showing ARP communications and warning signals, the other a plan of all the streets, open spaces etc. On the second map little coloured flags were used to follow the operations in an emergency.

A dart board, pin table, and other indoor pastimes had been provided for the staff to pass the time, and camp beds and blankets were in readiness for temporary sleeping quarters.

Miners were also sandbagging their shelters, specially built for protecting workers. All the pits in the area had been given instructions for defensive measures. Barnsley Main boasted that within one minute forty seconds of an air raid warning the surface workers, both men and women, would be in shelter – remarkably the time allowed for men in the pithead baths to complete their dress and for the winding engine men to complete their winds. Each employee was assigned his or her shelter, and to assist those who had to negotiate steps, slides where fitted to make evacuation easier. Obstacles such as tubs and rails were painted white, as were the shelters themselves. All eleven shelters had letters painted on the sides and front for clear identification. Each shelter was built to identical plans. At each end was a one-foot thick concrete wall, which guarded the entrance before a descent of steps which took the miner to an iron door. Within the concrete-floored shelter were seven steel arches, holding up the concrete roof. A lavatory, wash bowl, first aid equipment, buckets of sand, water and lime completed the assembly. On shift duty there was a full complement of air raid wardens, firefighting units, first aid posts and men drawn from the colliery ambulance workers, decontamination squads etc.

Men at Barnsley Main sandbagging the entrance to their air-raid shelter.

Most pits in Barnsley had similar precautions and the Borough Engineer's department pushed ahead with its plans so that four weeks after the outbreak of hostilities Barnsley had 600 public shelters, 1,823 basement shelters, 2,500 trench shelters, 1,950 deep shelters and 500 Anderson shelters.

Further out in Hoyland the first public shelters were being built on Tinker Lane, Hoyland Common and Market Street. Permanent warden's posts and thirteen public shelters had been established at Hoyland, Hoyland Common, Elsecar and Platts Common. Like in Barnsley, the posts were brick built with concrete roofs. The central control room with five telephones for ARP was at the rear of the Town Hall. A well-equipped first aid post at the Miners' Welfare Hall had been set up and was run by Dr Fairclough, assisted by Mrs Fairclough and Mrs Allott.

Group I, Sector 3, of Barnsley's civil defence wardens that had been assigned to Kendray in 1942. (courtesy of Mrs Catherine Laybourn)

WARDENS' POSTS

Air raid wardens' posts have been established at the following places within the County Borough:—A Group, stable, Bambridge's Yard, Church Street; B, No. 19 room, Girls' High School, and Wilthorpe Hotel garage; C, classroom at rear of Carlton Church Schools; D, room at rear of Wesleyan Reform Church, Smithies, and garage at New Lodge Estate Post Office; E, Highways Depot, High Street, Monk Bretton; F, basement of Lundwood Church, and pill box at Klondyke (Tumbling Lane on Barnsley—Monk Bretton road); G, Thompsons' Garage, Cundy Cross, and class room at Bethel Chapel, Hoyle Mill; H, Ardsley Police Station, and pill box at Highways Depot, Stanley Street; I, wash-house at Kendray Hotel; J, Wash-house at Junction Hotel, Doncaster Road and Cemetery Road; K, pill box, Avon Street, near Highways Depot, junction of Osborne Street; L, pill box, junction of Mount Vernon Road and Sheffield Road; M, at present in building at rear of Coach and Horses Hotel, Sheffield Road; N, garage at rear of Cross Keys Hotel, May Day Green; O, pill box, Town End Park; P, pill box adjoining Blackburn Lane Infants' School, and pill box, Victoria Crescent West; Q, pill box at junction of Agnes Road and Wood Street, and pill box on No. 1 allotment, California Gardens, Park Road; R, class room, St. Edward's School; S, 104, Dodworth Road, and pill box on Ring Road, Upper Dodworth Road; T, room in Greenwood Terrace at the back of Co-operative Society's funeral undertaking shop; U, pill box near North Eldon Street Schools.

Location of the warden posts in the town.

A decontamination centre was available at the council's depot on West Street. The Auxiliary Fire Service had three trailer pumps stationed No.1 AFS station near the Town Hall and at AFS Station, Tinker Lane.

Crossing back over the Dearne to Staincross, a former doctor's house on Church Street, Barnsley, was made into a strongpoint of Staincross civil defence. In it lodged the officers of the Staincross Area Joint Committee and the HQ of the Staincross ARP sub-controller and his staff.

ONE OF THESE IS YOUR NEAREST FIRE STATION:—

ADDRESS.		TELEPHONE	
Churchfield	....	Barnsley	2222
Fairfield	....	Barnsley	3140
Truelove's Garage, Wakefield Road	....	Barnsley	3364
Cundy Cross, Thompson's Garage	....	Barnsley	3461
Yorks. Traction Co., Upper Sheffield Rd.		Barnsley	3540
Perseverance Street	....	Barnsley	3478
Worsbro' Hall	....	Worsbro'	2245
Stocksbridge Fire Station	....	Stocksbridge	3148
Cudworth Fire Station	....	Cudworth	62
Darton Fire Station	....	Darton	139
Dodworth Fire Station	....	Silkstone	224
Royston	....	Royston	76
Wortley	....	Ecclesfield	38222

In case of emergency don't dial 999. Local numbers for the fire brigade had to be published. It wasn't until 1946 that 999 was introduced in Barnsley.

The ARP controller's Staincross office at the junction of Church Street and Old Mill Lane. On the left is Captain Peter Symons, the Staincross area controller.

COUNTY BOROUGH OF BARNSLEY

AIR RAID PRECAUTIONS

BABIES' ANTI-GAS HELMETS

DEMONSTRATIONS IN THE USE AND CARE OF BABIES' ANTI GAS HELMETS ARE HELD AT THE FOLLOWING CLINICS :—

BARNSLEY:
NEW STREET MEDICAL SERVICES CLINIC
MONDAY & THURSDAY AFTERNOONS—2.30 to 3.30 p.m.

CARLTON:
PARISH HALL, CHURCH STREET
MONDAY AFTERNOONS—2.30 p.m.

LUNDWOOD:
METHODIST CHAPEL, HAROLD AVENUE
TUESDAY AFTERNOONS—2.30 p.m.

ARDSLEY:
EBENEZER CHAPEL, HUNNINGLEY LANE, STAIRFOOT
WEDNESDAY MORNINGS—10.30 to 11.30 a.m.

MONK BRETTON:
HIGH STREET
FRIDAY MORNINGS—10.30 to 11.30 a.m.

MOTHERS OF CHILDREN under eighteen months who have not already been provided with a Helmet, are urged TO ATTEND AT ONE OF THE CLINICS detailed above, where they will be instructed in the use and care of the Anti-Gas Helmet. When the demonstrators are satisfied that the mothers know how to use these Helmets, a certificate will be issued to them entitling them to obtain a Helmet from the Central A.R.P. Stores, Peel Street, Barnsley, upon application.

Town Hall, Barnsley.
19th April, 1940.

A. E. GILFILLAN,
Town Clerk and Controller.
1365

Adverts like this encouraged new mums to be prepared.

As for the 'Barnsley Mountain', the continuously burning heap of muck, this had received some attention over the previous weeks. Water at 120 gallons per minute was pumped from the canal and pushed through 6-inch pipes onto the burning slag, damping down the glow.

On September 23 the *Barnsley Chronicle* printed a series of silhouettes of German planes courtesy of *The Aeroplane* magazine, for rapid recognition.

'Courageous Barnsley Lad' was a fitting tribute in the *Chronicle* to 20-year-old Royal Marine George Renshaw of 66 Rowland Road, Wilthorpe. George joined the Marines at 18 and was serving on the carrier *Courageous* at the start of the war with 811 and 822 squadrons, each equipped with a dozen Fairey Swordfish.

George Renshaw of Wilthorpe survivor of the aircraft carrier Courageous.

Courageous departed Plymouth on 3 September 1939 for an anti-submarine patrol in the Western Approaches escorted by four destroyers. On the evening of 17 September 1939 off the coast of Ireland, two of her four escorting destroyers had been sent to help a merchant ship under attack, all her aircraft had returned from patrols, and *Courageous* was stalked for two hours by *U-29* commanded by Captain Lieutenant Otto Schuhart. The carrier turned into the wind to launch her aircraft, putting the ship across the bow of the submarine, which fired three torpedoes. Two struck the ship before any aircraft took off and she capsized sinking in twenty minutes with the loss of 519 of her crew including her captain; 218 survivors were rescued. Two escorting destroyers then chased *U-29* for four hours but the submarine escaped. When the torpedoes struck, George was on sentry duty on deck and was violently thrown off his feet. The captain, William Totfield Makeig-Jones, who incidentally was born at Wath-upon-Dearne, gave the order to abandon ship within five minutes of contact, with the ship listing heavily. George discarded his clothes except his underwear and swam to another ship 200 yards away. He had won two swimming cups while with the Marines. Safely on board George was given a tot of rum, and when ashore was given eggs, steak and chips. Marine George Newsome of Hemsworth was not as fortunate as Marine Renshaw: he died when the ship exploded.

'Courageous Barnsley Lad' was a fitting tribute to one of Barnsley's first war casualties, 20-year-old Royal Marine George Renshaw of Wilthorpe.

Not a consequence of war but nevertheless another sad death happened on 28 September when the legendary master butcher and father of the Barnsley Chop, Albert Hirst, died at 62. It was reported that he was a very generous man and during the Great War his kindly acts, always given unostentatiously, were recognised by the Barnsley battalions. He left a wife, three sons, John, James and Albert, and countless others to mourn his passing.

HIRST'S
APPETISING SPECIALITIES

Freshly Shredded BEEF SUET PER 1/- LB.

Milk Fed CHICKENS From - 1/2 Per lb.

Prime Beef From Selected Animals, bred and fed on the Best Pastures to ensure tenderness and flavour, and hygienically slaughtered in the Modern Corporation Abattoir

AYLESBURY Ducklings PER 1/3 LB.

Hirst's Delicious Mincemeat PER 10d. LB.

ALBERT HIRST
CHEAPSIDE — BARNSLEY
telephones: 2294 and 3331

Albert Hirst, the famous butcher who died in the first month of the war.

Beer duty increased to a penny a pint and cigarette duty to a penny on twenty, a further pinch to already cash-strapped miners.

The nightly blackouts, whose times were printed weekly, and the consequent peril of crossing streets, explains why many Barnsley folk were cultivating the pleasures of inglenook and other parlour games, which had dwindled in popularity during the interwar years. J. Lodge & Sons on Eldon Street was happy to provide 'all kinds of games for winter evenings'.

In early October it was announced that the 215,000 'twenties' registered nationally a few months earlier would be remaining with their battalions; in Barnsley this amounted to 1,411 men. It was announced that the Barnsley twenties had been granted special leave at Christmas, perhaps to be the last one enjoyed by some of the soldiers and their families.

Barnsley's unemployment fell in October, bucking the trend nationally. This was partly due to the government's call to increase coal output by at least 30 million tons per year to 260 million tons. Some collieries in the Barnsley area reopened to meet the demand, including the Silkstone Fall Colliery after a closure of thirteen months; 120 men were taken on.

By now 2,000 infant respirators had been delivered to Barnsley. The 'deep sea diving'-looking gas masks were for children up to two years old. Parents placed their baby inside the mask so that the head was inside the steel helmet and the baby could see through the visor. Then they wrapped the canvas part around the baby's body with the straps fastened under its bottom like a nappy, its legs dangling free below. The canvas had a rubber coating to stop gas seeping through. There was an asbestos filter on the side to absorb poisonous gases. Attached to this was a rubber tube shaped like a concertina with a handle: this was pushed back and forth to pump air into the mask. Health visitors and child welfare centres gave lessons on how to use the mask. Despite instruction courses, few parents were entirely happy with encasing their child in an airtight chamber. In fact, there was some question over its safety. During demonstrations there were reports that babies fell asleep and became unnaturally still inside the masks! It is likely that sometimes the pump didn't push enough air into the mask and the babies came close to suffocating. Gas-proof prams were also available.

Dancing could still be enjoyed at the Baths Hall on Race Street every Saturday night and the cinemas were all still open, normally opening with a Pathé newsreel with the latest war news. Barnsley was considered a 'safe zone', safe enough for Barnsley to play a friendly against Leeds United at Oakwell, this following a 2-1 defeat to Halifax Town in a previous friendly watched by 3,000 fans.

In the First World War, Barnsley PALs were recruited together, trained together, moved to the south of France, went over to Egypt together, and eventually shared a dreadful fate on the Somme. The Second World War was different in that recruited soldiers were allocated to understrength regiments and dispersed all over the British Army. Nineteen-year-old Harry Killingbeck of Hoyle Mill joined the forces just before the war. He describes everything as being 'OK with nothing to worry about, we are billeted at a café, and since being attached to headquarters, we've dined like lords'. After finishing 'work', as he describes it, 'there is not much to do, there are no pictures or anything here, and the streets are filthy with mud.'

Another soldier from Barnsley serving in the Royal Army Ordnance Corps gave an indication of conditions in a letter to his mum:

We had quite a good crossing over here, the sea was very calm, and we are stationed in a nice little French port. We are sleeping in bunks, complete with mattress and pillow.

It is very interesting watching the French people. The peasants take all their washing to the river and wash their clothes on stone slabs on the river bank. All the people seem to have very clean clothes; even the poor children playing in the streets. The French people are very kind to us and they help us all they can, but very few speak English. We make each other understand with signs and sketches.

The French 'fags' are awful things to smoke and one cannot get English fags in France. I got a good stock of Woodbines off an English boat. The French bread is grand stuff to eat but the crusts are very hard. Things are very cheap here. I have changed £2 into French money and I feel just like a millionaire.

I am having a good holiday at the moment, and the weather is perfect... and don't worry.

Notice how he describes it as a 'holiday'!

History records this period as the 'Phoney War' – an eight-month period at the start of the war during which there were no major military land operations on the Western Front. It began with the German invasion of Poland on 1 September 1939 and ended with the German attack on France and the Low Countries on 10 May 1940, after which the Barnsley Home Guard, along with the corporation, dismantled and removed street names to confuse any invading Germans.

By late October 73,000 ration books had been written up for the town and were posted by early November to be used starting 8 January 1940. Only two foods had been rationed at this point: bacon (including ham) and butter, 4oz per person per week. The householder had to write the name of their preferred bacon and butter shops, and on page 3 of the book with coupons, the householder wrote their name and address. On page 4 the same process was followed; the shopkeeper then wrote or stamped his name on the counterfoil. Shops that sold butter or bacon engaged in a marketing campaign to tempt customers to ration with them.

Anne Hawkins of Cudworth's ration book was blue and her younger sister's was green and because of this they were allowed extra 'goodies'. Word always spread fast if there were extra rations at a shop.

Right and below: This War Office booklet was issued to the Home Guard to easily identify Germans and their tactics.

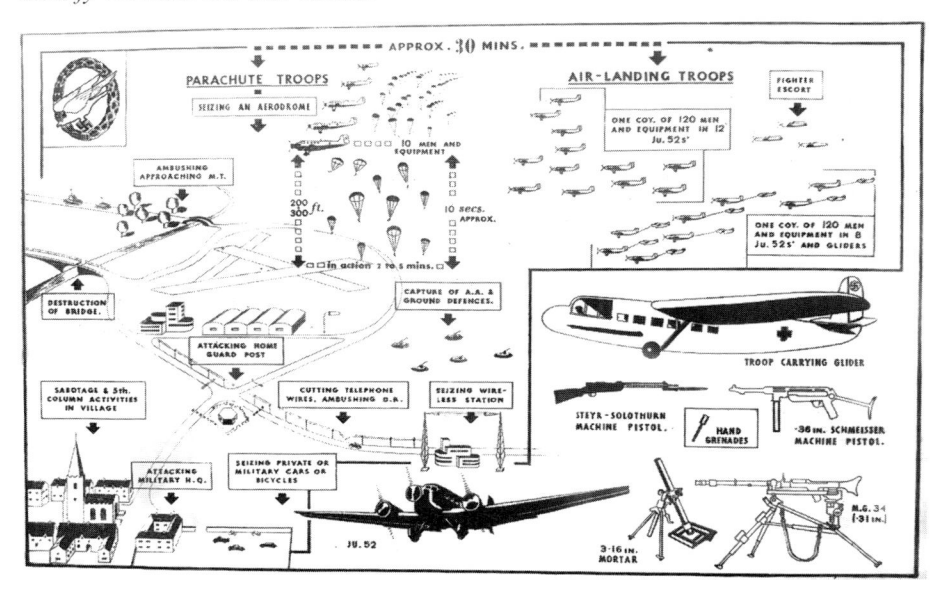

To get the ration books ready, sixty unemployed Barnsley people had been engaged through the Employment Exchange to supplement the volunteers and teachers. Special thanks was given to the vigilant work of the Women's Voluntary Service.

The WVS for Civil Defence was brought into being in 1938 by the then Home Secretary, Samuel Hoare. In Barnsley the WVS centre was opened in May 1938 on Eldon Street and since then and up to October 1939, 515 women had volunteered under the direction of Evelyn Gilfillan, wife of the Town Clerk, Eric. One role of the WVS was to recruit volunteers, advise them as to which branch of the service they were most suited, and hand them onto the local authority to be trained, ensuring that no one was overlooked. Evelyn retired from this role in June 1942 after seeing the service evolve into an association of 1,200 women. This was a women's war as much as a man's. WVS was also inaugurated at Dodworth, Darfield and Worsbrough Dale. Evelyn was succeeded by Mrs A. Bunting.

Barnsley had the oldest and youngest members of the WVS in Great Britain. Miss Elizabeth Hoyland of 60 Limesway was 102 and Miss Mary Carter of Southwell Street was 13. Although 16 was the official age to join, the authorities made an exception for Mary who was in hospital and wanted something worthwhile to do. Barnsley's distinction was revealed through the BBC in *Women at War*. Elizabeth died in December 1943 at the home of her great niece.

The canteen department of the ARP services (ARP personnel in Barnsley had two shillings per day food allowance) was in the capable hands of two WVS officers. Four other WVS volunteers helped at the child welfare clinics and helped Dr Tomlin at the Ear and Eye clinic. Although not civil defense as such, it did alleviate the pressures on existing staff.

Leading up to the war, women had been busy knitting blankets and asking members of the public to knit six-inch squares to stitch together. The resulting blankets were sent to Skipton and other receiving

Here are the oldest and youngest workers for Barnsley WVS: Elizabeth Hoyland of 60 Limesway, and Mary Carter of Southwell Street, Barnsley.

areas in Yorkshire where the needs of evacuated children was urgent. These women worked tirelessly during the war – in 1942 Barnsley WVS dispatched 1,420 parcels to soldiers – and they received many letters of thanks.

Women's Institutes and other patriotic ladies held knitting circles, influenced by slogans such as, 'If you can knit — you can do your bit'. Knitting patterns were printed called 'War Knitting' and the Sirdar Wool Company produced wool specially dyed in service colours, i.e. khaki, navy blue, and Air Force blue and grey. They knitted pullovers with long sleeves, sleeveless pullovers, gloves, balaclavas and other garments which were 'lovely, cosy and warm'.

Private William Roper, 4686527, Duke of Wellington's (West Riding) Regiment, who died aged 28 on 14 October 1939 was reputed to be the first British soldier to be killed in France in the war. William was the son of Peter and Jane Roper of West Town, Dewsbury, but William spent the first fourteen years of his life in Barnsley and was born on New Street. His father Peter was employed at Barnsley Main Colliery where he died in an accident. Before moving to Dewsbury with his mother to start a new life, William lived at Marine Row, Racecommon Road. He was a collier before the outbreak of the war and served as a reservist, spending some time in India. In France he belonged to a labour company, in which he had served little more than three weeks before he was killed. The last letter his mother received came on the day he was killed and spoke of his excellent state of health and the good time he was having. He died of drowning, accidently falling into some water. William is remembered at the Janval Cemetery, Dieppe. His CO wrote to Mrs Nicholls, 'I feel sure you will be proud to know that as the first British soldier to be killed during this war, he was buried with full military honours.' (CC 4 Nov 1939)

'The Cliffe' residence of Mrs Lancaster resembled a miniature post office just before Christmas in preparation for parcels to be sent to Barnsley servicemen from Monk Bretton, Smithies and Old Mill from Miss Lancaster's 'League of Comforts' fund. A lady's sewing party had been meeting at the 'Cliffe' each week since September 1939 knitting socks, helmets, scarves and mittens and each lady made a personal contribution towards the much-welcomed goods. Each parcel, valued at about ten shillings, contained knitted woollen garments, stationery, books, shaving soap, toilet soap, sardines, chewing gum, handkerchief, toffee, chocolate, cigarettes and a Christmas card which read: 'from the Misses Lancaster and all your friends at Monk Bretton'. Similar arrangements were set up throughout the district.

Incidentally the Lancasters were a well-known family in Monk Bretton. Alice Hilda Lancaster was a nurse who died in the Great War and the news was reported in the *Barnsley Chronicle*: 'Much regret was expressed in Barnsley on

A woman voluntary worker sorts some of the hundreds of packs of playing cards, woollens and footballs – more 'comforts' for the troops.

Wednesday at the receipt of the news of the death of Miss Alice Hilda Lancaster, youngest daughter of Mr Thos Lancaster JP of Cliffe House, Monk Bretton, who had been on hospital work in France. Miss Lancaster, who was drowned while bathing with a friend, had only been overseas for about a week. Since October 1916 she had been on the nursing staff of St Thomas's Hospital, London and prior to that period was on the nursing staff at Lundwood Military Hospital. The deceased lady, who was 35 years of age, was well known, and had been prominently engaged on social work.' Alice Hilda Lancaster's grave is in Wimereux Communal Cemetery, near Boulogne.

Captain Bingley Lancaster of Cliffe House led the Monk Bretton Home Guard Company which had their headquarters at the Girl Guides and Boy Scouts building which later became the Redfearn Sports and Social Club.

Recycling is not a new age phenomenon: early on during hostilities people had been encouraged to leave tin and paper next to their usual waste for the local council to recycle. Townsfolk 'did their bit' and their waste was put to effective use at the Pogmoor Refuse Works, formerly the old brick works. At these works, the second plant to be installed in England in the 1920s, refuse was screened and sorted. A revitalised workforce under the aptly-named foreman Mr J. Tipping baled newspaper and cardboard in their new baling machine.

Converting tin into 'gold' another process. All the tin was placed in a trough before the lid was closed and heat was applied, resulting in condensed 12-inch square cubes of useful metal. From September 1939 to March 1940 the council had salvaged 156 tons of paper, 61 tons of tin and 48 tons of glass.

The local authority also issued appeals to save waste foodstuffs for pigs, oyster and similar shells to produce grit, other metals, textiles, bottles and string. Grease and bones were required to extract fat for the manufacture of glue for aircraft.

December saw the testing of air raid sirens and local ARP groups holding demonstrations, drills and practicing for the worst. It was reported that each area excelled due to thorough planning and preparation. Another event of note was the

COUNTY BOROUGH OF BARNSLEY.

EMERGENCY POWERS (DEFENCE).

THE CONTROL OF PAPER (No. 1) ORDER, 1939, MADE BY THE MINISTER OF SUPPLY UNDER THE DEFENCE REGULATIONS, 1939.

NOTICE IS GIVEN that the **Reclamation of Used Paper, Cardboard, Wrapping Paper and Cardboard Boxes** is now a vital necessity to provide Supplies for Re-manufacture and replace imports of Wood Pulp, etc. Paper and Cardboard are essential for War and Industry.

HOUSEHOLDERS are requested **NOT** to place their Waste Paper in the Dust-bin, but to **WRAP IT IN A BUNDLE AND PLACE IT ALONGSIDE THE DUSTBIN FOR COLLECTION BY THE REFUSE COLLECTORS.**

TRADESMEN AND SHOPKEEPERS are requested to Ask the Cleansing Department, Town Hall, Barnsley, to collect their Waste Paper.

(Signed) A. E. GILFILLAN,
Town Hall.   Town Clerk.
Barnsley.   21/9/39   3979

Above: Recycling notice issued by the council in 1939.

Right: This picture shows the men at Pogmoor handling a bale of waste paper collected in response to the recycling drive.

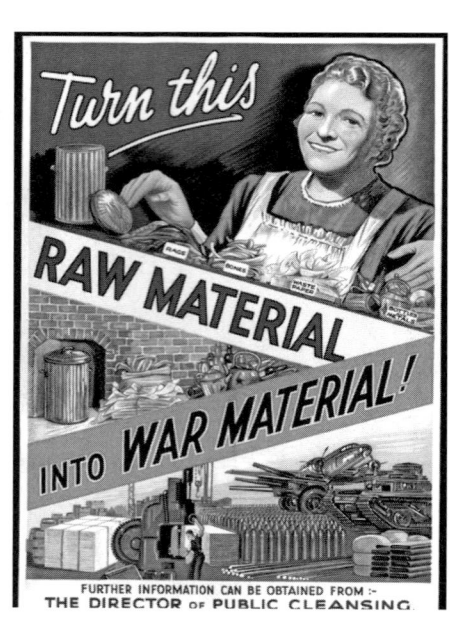

Above left and right: Householders were encouraged to save anything they could to help the war effort.

setting up by Mayor George Mason of the Barnsley War Services Fund with gifts donated to the Town Hall.

Still in December the next group of 'twenties' – those who were 20, 21 or 22 on the 1st of December but had not reached their 23rd birthday – were required to enrol at the employment office; 1,521 registered in this batch including 7 conscientious objectors.

Conscientious objectors found themselves ostracised – even within their own families and immediate neighbours. Religious or political convictions prevented most from committing to the Armed Forces. Albert Schroeder, the leader of Jehovah's Witnesses, was deported back to the USA, and ordinary men and women were imprisoned. William Scholey and Joseph Pallet of Worsbrough Bridge were given six months hard labour. Pallet said, 'there is a higher authority than man that we must obey,' as he referred to the bible texts of loving thy neighbour and thou shall not kill. Nancy Pallett of St Mary's Place even refused to work as a bus conductress and was fined.

Others from Barnsley made the headlines: Lewis Potts, 26, of Bridge Street was removed from the list of objectors after he admitted joining the Jehovah's Witnesses just after the outbreak of the war so he didn't have to fight.

Defense Regulation 18B of August 1939 had suspended the right of *Habeas Corpus* for the first time since the Magna Carta. This allowed the government

British Union detainees in front of barbed wire fence, Isle of Man, 1941: far left, George 'Bert' Brocklebank, of Barnsley.

to imprison people without charge. The politically motivated British Union was one victim of this legislation: more than a thousand Unionists were detained on the Isle of Man, including members Freddy Firth and George 'Bert' Brocklebank.

Stoker Jack Harrison, RN, from Worsbrough Bridge was the first sailor living in Barnsley to die in the war. Twenty-year-old Jack, a former pupil of Worsbrough Dale National School, sailed for China on 1 September 1938 on the destroyer *Duchess* which collided with another British warship. On the declaration of war a flotilla of nine ships, all 'D' Class destroyers, were ordered to leave their Chinese port and sail for the UK with 'the greatest possible speed'. It was an impressive and morale-boosting sight for the crew of the *Duchess* as they had steamed away in single file at thirty knots, refuelling at Singapore, then passing Colombo, Aden and the Suez Canal. At Malta, three of the destroyers, *Duchess*, *Dainty* and *Delight* were detailed to escort the 31,000-ton *Barham* from Gibraltar to Scotland. It had been a lightning trip, the fastest east-west passage ever recorded. The *Duchess* was only one hour from her dock at Greenock and most of the crew were below asleep. The petty officer on watch had closed down all but

Stoker Jack Harrison, RN, from Worsbrough Bridge was the first sailor living in Barnsley to have died in a theatre of war.

Your own vegetables all the year round... if you **DIG FOR VICTORY NOW**

Posters like these encouraged the town's people to seek out any plot of land and use it to grow their own food to supplement their rations.

one of the gunnery emplacements. He held a roll-call of his ten-gun crew and ordered them to go below to secure their hammocks and to clear the way for their messmates at breakfast. There was a blackout and no moonlight. He adjusted his headphones and looked aft. It was then that he saw the massive shape of a ship's prow bearing down on him out of the darkness. It towered over the diminutive destroyer and with a sickening sound it hit the *Duchess* amidships at such speed that she simply turned over. Some men dived into the icy oily sea as other half-naked sailors scrambled desperately around the rolling hull. The *Barham*'s searchlight lit up the scene – it had been her towering form that had pushed the *Duchess* over. The screws were still turning as her horrified crew swept the sea for survivors. There had been no time to grab lifebelts. Of 145 men on board only one officer and 22 ratings survived.[13]

Harry Hughes of 25 Market Street, Cudworth, was on board the heavy cruiser HMS *Cumberland* and experienced the bitter battle with the *Graf Spee* at the Battle of the River Plate, the first major naval battle in the Second World War. Harry left the Cudworth Modern School under the mastership of Ed Lightowler at the age of 14 and joined the Royal Navy, passing all his exams after six months achieving distinctions in rifle shooting and heavy gun activities. At just 17 Harry was a relative veteran of the sea.

Christmas 1939 in Barnsley seemed different to celebrations in the past. 'Peace on earth and goodwill to all men' seemed a mockery of the Yuletide spirit when Christian men had been killing other Christian men, women and children in Europe. Those on leave, in their khaki, RAF blue and navy blue uniforms, all speaking tales of adventure, would have been a welcome sight. Christmas trade was brisk, and the clement weather lent itself to a bustling town centre.

Food rationing officially started on 8 January 1940. Regulating the consumption of food was considered an infringement of rights by some, but most considered it a necessity to help win the war. Adverts appeared on bill boards and in local newspapers telling people to avoid the unnecessary. It was reported on the last weekend in January that the town had run out of meat: a Sunday lunch without meat would not have gone down well in Barnsley. Ham and bacon were rationed, but other meats were still being supplied to butchers based on the number of people they had registered.

Barnsley welcomed the cold New Year with a scandal so bad it made the headlines of national newspapers. Barnsley's twenty-one head wardens of the ARP all resigned and in a statement issued to the press they protested that their suggestions were being ignored and the 'sweeping changes' that had been made where 'not in the interests of an efficient service'. A public spat ensued between the head wardens and the Emergency Committee, who argued that although the statement from the wardens included the names of the wardens, only one person had signed it. The wardens vehemently denied this. A bluff was called when the committee declared that all the vacancies would be filled by civic-minded individuals, and on Monday, 22 January, the head wardens met at the Three Cranes Hotel and resolved to meet with the Emergency Committee to discuss what they described as 'an awkward situation'. The head wardens eventually were replaced.

An appeal went out to youngsters to curb their mischievous behaviour as it seems that having fathers away was an excuse for some to misbehave. One 15-year-old lad was charged with stealing whisky, gin, brandy, sherry and cigarettes, the property of members of the Barnsley Club, Regent Street. He had been recruited to the ever-growing army of 'spivs' selling illicit goods on the black market. The boy was ordered to join the RAF scouts.

Three other schoolboys, 11, 12 and 13, pled guilty to attempting to steal a packet of cigarettes from George White of Charles Street who had business premises on Sheffield Road.

It seems stealing cigarettes was in vogue. In Darfield a 10- and a 13-year-old schoolboy had been charged with stealing fifty fags, two cinema tickets and 7s 6d

The Barnsley Scouts outside the Town Hall during the St Georges Day parade. These lads would play a vital part in the war as runners for the various civil defence organisations.

from the till of Cordelia Coe's shop on Snape Hill. These little Artful Dodgers also asked three other cases to be considered: stealing an electric bicycle lamp, 2lbs of chocolates, and breaking and entering the Coop at Darfield to steal a cake. Both boys pled guilty and were fined.

Several children got into trouble for damaging air raid shelters, including nicking the keys. One boy just 9 was ordered to pay 8s 6d for damaging two key boxes in the Baker Street ARP shelter and 15s damages for stealing the two keys.

Juvenile crime increased every year during the war.

Reality struck when 19-year-old Private Clifford Mills was the first soldier with his home in town to die on the Western Front. He was the son of Henry Mills of Back South Street off Dodworth Road and died of wounds received in action. Clifford joined the Y&L two years before the war and before that worked as a 'takerin' at Redfearn's. His brother Norman was also in the forces with the KOYLI.

Sergeant Pilot Jack Ramshaw (562599) was the first person from Barnsley and district to be awarded the Distinct Flying Medal. Jack, from Penistone, was the son of A. Ramshaw, manager of Penistone Labour Exchange who served in the First World War in the submarine service. Jack took off in Wellington bomber N9283 at

Above left: Clifford Mills, the first soldier from the town to die on the Western Front from wounds.

Above right: Jack Ramshaw from Penistone was the first person from Barnsley and district to be awarded the DFM.

0900 hours with eight other 9 Squadron Wellingtons from RAF Honington to carry out a reconnaissance in the Schilling/Jade Road and Wilhelmshaven to attack any battleships or cruisers. His Wellington flew in formation with nine aircraft from 149 and 37 squadrons, reaching Wilhelmshaven after being harried for quite some time. After leaving Wilhelmshaven the Wellingtons were followed for 70/80 miles to the German coast by enemy fighters. Using the experimental Freya radar system, the bomber force was tracked from a radar base on Wangerooge. N9283 was so badly beaten up it crashed into the North Sea at 1530 hours near Cromer Knoll. Four of the injured crew were picked up by a trawler and one of the men was taken to hospital in Grimsby; the three others returned to RAF Honington in Suffolk. Jack received the DFM and was Penistone's first 'hero'.

During April, Barnsley was busy sending parcels to the servicemen, with comfort funds being registered at all local district councils and women's groups including the women's branch of the British Legion, whose new headquarters was at the Old Windmill Hotel, Shambles Street. Hundreds of appreciative letters were received weekly.

There was also an appeal from the Chief Constable, Mr H.T. Williams, for 250 men to volunteer for the AFS. On joining up and after passing a medical the men would have had training in firefighting, gas, high explosives and incendiary bombs. The commander in 1940 was Mr J. C. Heppenstall and Mr A. Briggs was the deputy commander.

Compulsory service had now caught up with the men of the '25' class; 1,800 had registered with five provisionally registering as conscientious objectors. It was also announced that men who passed fit at grade 3 were now being called up; this would include men with minor eyesight defects.

Volunteers from Barrow Colliery just before decontamination drill near the pit.

Left: Police officers inspecting one of six pumps which had been installed at the fire station for use by auxiliary firemen under the ARP.

A positive effect of the war in Barnsley was the industrial development and consequent work for the town. Barnsley was on the list of subcontractors for government work and some subcontracts had already been received from the Ministry of Supply by March 1940. But the phoney war had now ended, austerity measures had taken hold, and Barnsley was now gripped by world events.

CHAPTER 3

The Phoney War Ends

Barnsley had *déjà vu* when Germany invaded the Low Countries and France on 10 May 1940. This coincided with the town's Whitsuntide celebrations which were subsequently cancelled. It was also announced that the Bank Holiday Monday was to be cancelled.

Almost immediately, refugees from Holland and Belgium were enthusiastically welcomed in Hoyland and Wombwell. All were anticipated to be billeted in public halls until accommodation could be found.

As jack boots crossed the border, soldiers from Barnsley braced themselves for Blitzkrieg, dislocating them from their units and battalions. Two soldiers, one from Dodworth and the other from Royston, escaped in a 'borrowed' boat from Norway. National headlines described how nine soldiers from northern regiments escaped with the help of two Norwegian naval lieutenants and made for home. Of

This was the first of two food vans provided to the local authority. This one was first used for school meals.

the nine, two came from Barnsley: Private Harry Green of Mitchelson Avenue, Dodworth, and Lieutenant Corporal Norman Frost of Newtown Avenue, Royston, both Y&L Regiment. After losing the main body of their unit, they made their way down to the coast via the mountains towards Grota, then changing into Norwegian civilian clothes and commandeering a cargo boat. Avoiding mines, German boats and aircraft, they managed to get back to England after seven days and 200 miles. Harry Green was presented with a gift of £4 7s 6d at the Horse and Jockey Hotel. Barnsley's first Great Escape!

Dad's Army on standby

An appeal went out for volunteers for the Local Defence Volunteers, later called the Home Guard. The appeals went out at 9 pm on Tuesday, 14 May and by 9.30 police in the County Borough office were engaged in registering volunteers. Nationally 250,000 volunteers registered in the first week and in the West Riding 35,000. The only fitness requirement was that they should be 'capable of free movement'.

So great was the response that on Wednesday evening the clerks had to work under 'high pressure' to fill out the forms. Men volunteered from all professions and trades – managers, dentists, organists, clerks, mine-workers, shop keepers

Home Guard machine gunners concealed and ready for the invaders.

THE PHONEY WAR ENDS   89

Members of the 1st Cadet Battalion, Y and L Regiment (Barnsley), rifle shooting teams. They are (left to right) back row: Lieutenant A.L. Senior, Corporal Hawksworth, B.Q.M.S Ibberson, Lieutenant C.P Brown, front row: Sergeant Watling, R.S.M. Green, Major H.J. McKenzie, Cadet Mathers and Cadet Hobson.

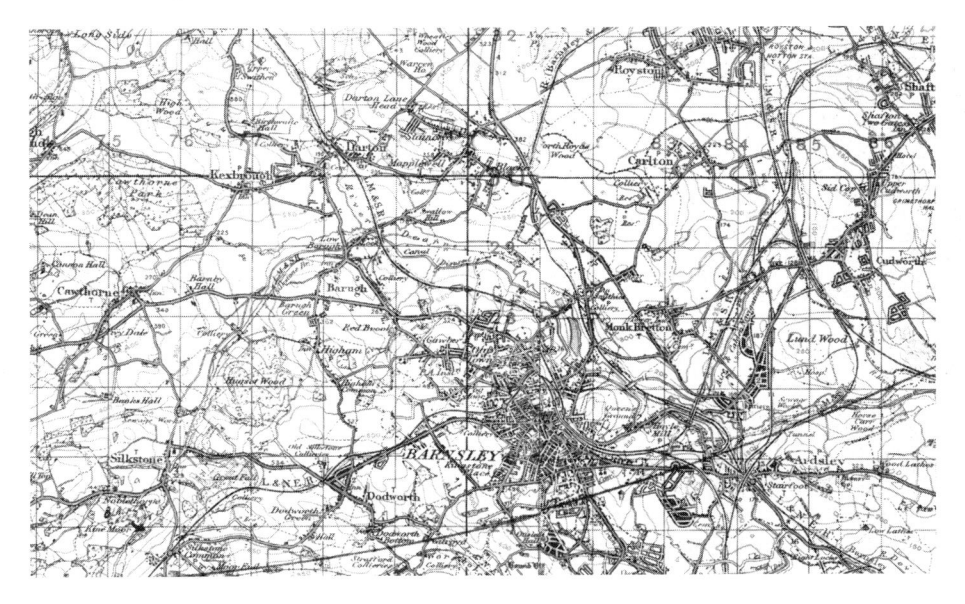

1940 Revision map of Barnsley. (author's collection)

and assistants, and the unemployed – and while many were youths of 17 to 19 and some in their 60s, the majority were in their 40s. By Friday, over 500 had volunteered either in the Barnsley office, or in Ardsley, Carlton or Monk Bretton.

Many had previous military experience and were already skilled in firearms, and all ranks up to major were represented, in addition to many naval ranks. One volunteer had served in the South African campaign. The volunteers were not paid, and in the early days few were equipped with rifles; on average one gun had to serve ten men.

Colonel James Walker would be the West Riding commandant, with ex-Chief Detective Superintendent William Huddlestone, who retired from the West Riding Constabulary at the end of 1938, his deputy. Commanders were appointed quickly for all but two of the twenty-three groups in the West Riding area, including Captain Hallam for Barnsley County and Major J.G.E. Rideal DSO for the County Borough. The West Riding area was part of Northern Command which included Northumbria, Yorkshire and the North Midland area.

In Hoyland, Shirley Parker remembers her Home Guard experience: 'A local Dad's Army was formed and practised every Sunday morning. I have never seen anything so funny in all my life. To simulate gunfire one member hammered on a dustbin lid and their guns were brooms with which they marched as smartly as they could, parading through the village. Sheffield, the heart of the steelworks, was a mere 9 miles away and tanks were being built at a factory about 4 miles away and the tanks were road tested through the village. The noise and dust they created was quite frightening at first.'

Sixteen battalions of Home Guard were affiliated to the York and Lancaster Regiment. They proudly wore the Tiger and Rose in their cap and on their battledress blouse was a curved shoulder title with the words 'Home Guard' and below it the letters WR (for West Riding) along with the Battalion number.

56th West Riding (Barnsley)
70th West Riding (Staincross)
71st West Riding (Staincross) (based at Cudworth)
72nd West Riding (Staincross) (based at Ward Green)

In May 1941, the Hallamshire Zone was extended to include the Barnsley and Staincross Groups and a further change was made in May 1943 when the Sheffield Group became the Hallamshire Sector, the Rotherham Group became the Rotherham Sector and the Barnsley and Staincross Groups became the Staincross Sector.

Barnsley Home Guard. (courtesy of Paul Wilkinson)

In addition, three anti-aircraft batteries were formed in 1942 from men who were transferred from the existing battalions. These were numbered WR101, WR105 and WR106.

Back on the front line, Royston soldier Ronald Stephens of the Coldstream Guards and youngest son of Mr R. Stephens of 55 Poplar Terrace had a harrowing experience fighting the Nazis first hand. Ronald related how he and his company had gone to hold up the Germans from the main body and it was 'like hell let loose'. His company was blown up by an enemy mechanised column which was like one 'mass of fire'. They managed to escape from the Germans joining up with some Belgian troops. It was then he was blown into a canal and lost all his clothes except his trousers. An ambulance unit found him and took him to hospital. On reaching the French hospital, Guardsman Stephens explained he was bombed by German planes. On the hospital ship on the way home he was bombed again. He added, 'it makes my blood boil to see helpless women and children and wounded soldiers receiving such treatment.'

Our boys at Dunkirk

Following Operation Dynamo, local news was peppered with reports of soldiers missing or killed in action.

Above: German troops scavenging the beaches at Dunkirk after the Allied retreat.

Below: Scores of abandoned tanks the Germans passed en route to Dunkirk.

Private Jack Beardsall, aged 20, of Park Road, was one of dozens of Barnsley men trapped on the infamous French beach. After a tense period of waiting on the shore at Dunkirk on 28 May he boarded a British destroyer, imagining that he was safe. But a torpedo from a German motor torpedo boat smacked into his ship, sinking it within 45 minutes. After some time in the cold English Channel clinging to wreckage, Jack swam towards another destroyer about half a mile away. Not quite making the swim Jack sought refuge on the half-sunken hull of a British ship. Next thing he saw was a British destroyer ramming a German submarine: that submarine was sliced in two. As dawn was breaking he set off to swim towards two incoming lifeboats, as the boats could not get close enough due to the swell. Unable to reach the lifeboat he eventually was picked up by a troop carrier. After reaching a port in Kent he travelled to Aldershot wrapped in just a blanket and with the food he was given in Kent. From Aldershot he was taken to a medical reception station where he enjoyed a thorough rest.

Private Jack Beardsall, one of many Barnsley men stuck on the beaches at Dunkirk.

Speaking in England after engaging the Germans at the Maginot Line, Barnsley hero Gunner William Barraclough of Dodworth Road summed up the British spirit when he declared, 'we had a hot time, but we're not licked yet – not by a long chalk.' Describing the retreat to the coast he said, 'things were bad enough, but they were a hundred times worse when the Belgian army surrendered on our flank. There was some terrific fighting to hold that end afterwards, and to cover our retreat to the only port left us – Dunkirk... Off and on I was doing rear guard during the whole retreat – practically from the time we arrived in front of Brussels on

Barnsley hero Gunner William Barraclough of Dodworth Road summed up the British spirit at Dunkirk when he gallantly declared, 'we had a hot time, but we're not licked yet – not by a long chalk.'

May 11 to the time we embarked at Dunkirk on Saturday.' William was clearly distressed by what he saw, including the indiscriminate bombing of women and children. The death of a young woman and her 5-week-old twins haunted him. Referring to the embarkation William said, 'It was hell on the beaches. The German artillery was shelling all night and the airmen bombing all day. The town was in ruins. We had to swim for it twice, and when we got aboard a destroyer we were bombed three times taking casualties. Then when we got almost to England a pleasure steamer which was acting as a transport collided with us and almost capsized us.'

Miss Mabel Beckett (later McCobb) of 'Oakwell', Broadway, Barnsley, who was a member of the Territorial Army Nursing Service, was also amongst those evacuated from the French seafront town.

It must have felt peculiar for the men returning from Dunkirk, which was essentially a defeat, coming back to a hero's welcome. Soldiers were invited to social events, presented with money and gifts, and invited to speak to the press. On Eldon Street the YMCA welcomed home and billeted returnees.

Yorkshire Traction buses that had been converted into ambulances at the outbreak of the war were used to transport casualties arriving at Sheffield to local hospitals including Becketts.

By July 1940 the number of men conscripted nationally was now 4,000,000 and the age reached was 33. A further appeal to women between the ages of 18 and 42 went out in July to register for the Auxiliary Territorial Service; every duty which the ATS undertook released a soldier for other war work. Women received two thirds the pay of male soldiers.

Further rationing started from 22 July. Butter and margarine was limited to 6oz, and fat, for example lard, was limited to 3oz.

With coal being at a premium, some collieries in the district were forced to issue summonses to miners who were in breach of contract by absenting themselves from work. Darfield Main Colliery had absenteeism due to a pay dispute. Twenty-one miners were summoned to the West Riding police court; they were fined 50 shillings plus costs. Similarly in Grimethorpe fifty-two miners had been summonsed. The consequences in this case were far more serious than at Darfield: as a protest 3,000 miners came out on a lightning strike which had no sanction from the leaders. By the end of 1942 Regional Investigation Officers had been appointed for monitoring absence.

Twenty thousand tons of coal were lost due to a week's strike, prompting Joseph Hall, president of the Yorkshire Mineworkers Association, to call for government control of the mining industry to expedite production. A new law which made strikes illegal came into force on 26 July, forcing the men and boys back to work.

An unusual order was issued in Barnsley in July: the Clearance of Lofts Order, 1940. It ordered householders to clear and keep clear all articles stored in lofts and attics which were not used for human habitation. This was done as a fire precaution and officers had powers of entry to inspect premises to ensure compliance. Any articles removed were not to be destroyed but made available for collection.

In August the Town Hall inaugurated a revolutionary broadcasting bulletin system with several members of the Local Information Committee delivering brief talks. The first announcement was made via speakers on Market Hill in front of the Town Hall at 5 pm. Traffic on the roads was 'fairly heavy' with footfall described as heavy. The purpose of the broadcast was to 'instruct, advise and inform the public in the event of normal communications failing owing to a severe air attack,' said Alderman Joseph Jones in his first broadcast. Jones used the platform to issue a rousing speech to those who could be bothered to stop and listen.

Barnsley welcomed the arrival of refugees from Jersey on 21 June 1940. They came all the way from Southampton by train. Later in the war the town formed a Barnsley Channel Islands Society. At their meetings, news of the islands and islanders was circulated and all the islanders in Barnsley and Wombwell were encouraged to join. Moving on three years, 500 Channel Islanders from South Yorkshire and Lancashire met at the Adult School, giving some indication of the hospitality afforded to the refugees, from the reception centres at the Ebenezer, Pitt Street and Blucher Street chapels and the churches of St Luke's and St Edward's. Special thanks were given to the billeting officer Mr A. Anderson. In Wombwell, equal gratitude was given to their billeting officer Mr C. Knowles.

The first wartime Barnsley feast week in August 1940 was curtailed due to the war effort. Shops still closed on the Monday and Tuesday, but collieries in the district limited the lay-off to just three days. Both the east and south coasts had been closed to holiday makers, forcing Yorkshire Traction to run excursions mainly to the west, with Blackpool the choice for most. Beauty spots within easy reach of Barnsley were all looking forward to increased custom for the extended weekend rather than the usual week off.

With the feast week in full swing the Home Guard were busy preparing for the worst. The Home Guard No. 1 Barnsley Borough Battalion B Company orders had been issued for the second and third week in August which again focused on machine-gun training and sentry drill. Sentry drill showed the men how to challenge anyone who approached by shouting, 'Halt! Who goes there? friend or foe?'

Halt! Who goes there? A Barnsley Home Guard soldier requests Adam Gilfillan's papers as the Mayor looks on. (Barnsley Chronicle)

September to December 1940

With the Battle of Britain raging in the skies above England, the Austrian potentate fixed his date for Operation Sea Lion, threatening Britain with his immortal words at a Berlin rally: 'When the British air force drops two or three or four thousand kilograms of bombs, then we will in one night drop 150, 230, 300 or 400 thousand kilograms - we will raze their cities to the ground.'

That speech was prompted by the bombing of Berlin by the RAF, which involved the men of Barnsley. A flight sergeant from the town, who unfortunately was not named in the source document, described his experiences: 'Once over Berlin I came down to 3,000 feet through a gap in the clouds. After waiting for 20 minutes I was just able to find the target – a power station. We bombed just off it, but other aircraft got it and caused some nice fires at the gasworks. There really is nothing to the Berlin trip. It's like riding a bike after a time or two.'

The Barnsley Spitfire appeal raised £237 in the first week, inspiring George Evans of Locke Park to pen this poem:

The Mayor, Jim Walton, with the Barnsley Auxiliary Fire Service 'C' Section at Cundy Cross. After a concert held at the Keel Inn, Stairfoot the men handed over £8 for the Spitfire fund. (Barnsley Chronicle)

Little coal-black Barnsley town,
Where for you in world renown?
In your townsfolk, smiling, gay,
Thus we see them every day.

They give to this, they give to that,
After giving - take round the hat,
Empty this, fill it once more,
Buy raffle tickets by the score.

Yes, dear Mayor - a Spitfire, you ask;
This is easy your townsfolk's task,
Now you've spoken, they know their duty,
Let's hope will prove a Barnsley beauty.

And, when on a bombers tail,
Will give the good old Barnsley hail,

98   BARNSLEY AT WAR 1939–45

Here you are! Take this! You blighter!
Who the heck named 'you' a fighter?

Down he'll come; on Spitfire go;
Barnsley people; know you so.
As they gave, so you will give -
Your life, perhaps, that they might live,

They're all alike, in this little borough,
Mason, clerk, collier, labourer;
Policy and Party count as nil,
It's Nazidom they're out to kill,

Unemployed and worker too,
Will contribute their bit to you,
Giving freely, their muckle or mickle,
To put old Hitler in a pickle.

To raise funds a 'Fighter Dance' was held at the Three Cranes Hotel. For 3 shillings the guests enjoyed a bar, buffet and music by Phil Thomson and his band.

HAVE YOU RESPONDED
To The Mayor's Call For **£5000**
TO PUT BARNSLEY'S SPITFIRE
INTO THE AIR IMMEDIATELY

The Boys of the **R.A.F.** are doing **THEIR** bit for you --- so rally round --- do **YOUR** bit for them

★ Help to break the Nazi Luftwaffe boast of arrogance, cruelty and ruthlessness and thus end a career of persecution.
★ Together with ONE ACCORD.
To Hesitate Delays Final Victory

DON'T DELAY -- DO IT NOW

THIS SPACE HAS BEEN GIVEN BY THE "BARNSLEY CHRONICLE" Ltd. TO HELP THE FUND

Raising money for the Mayor's Spitfire fund in 1940.

THE PHONEY WAR ENDS

James Joseph 'Orange' O'Meara whose father worked as a sanitary inspector for the council.

A fund-raising committee was formed in the Shafton, Grimethorpe and Brierley area composed of all shopkeepers and club stewards, another by Dr Fairclough in Hoyland, another in the Lundwood district under the stewardship of Mr F.G. Robinson, and one in Cudworth.

Dances, fêtes, jumble sales etc. had been organised in almost village and town around Barnsley to raise money for the Spitfire. Every week in the *Chronicle* the Mayor's fund was printed showing their efforts.

Some servicemen who joined the RAF had been mentioned in dispatches. Corporal William Sykes, 20, a fitter in the air force, was 15 when he joined the RAF from Barnsley Technical College as an aircraft apprentice, and before that was a scholar at Grove Street and Raley schools.

A famous pilot of the time was James Joseph 'Orange' O'Meara whose father worked as sanitary inspector for the council. James was born in Barnsley in 1919 and was certified as a pilot, piloting a Gypsy Moth, in 1937. Entering the RAF on short commission in April 1938 at the age of 19, he was confirmed as a pilot officer on 4 April 1939. On 18 June he was posted to 9 FTS, RAF Hullavington, and while there obtained his first kill, over Dunkirk on 31 May 1940 when he brought down a Bf 109. He had already damaged a Ju 88 off Calais on 21 May. His next claim was a Bf 109 of JG 51, shot down in flames over the English Channel on 19 July, and ten days later, while intercepting a raid over Dover, claimed two Ju 87s. On 11 August he claimed 2 Bf 109 'probables' and on the following day destroyed one more. He claimed a Bf 109 down on 13 August, on the 15th he damaged three Heinkel He 111 bombers, and on the 18th he claimed an He 111 and shared destruction of a Ju 88. O'Meara was shortly afterwards posted to No. 72 Squadron at Biggin Hill and on 3 September was promoted to flying officer, before damaging a Do 17 on 27 September. He was awarded a DFC on 24 September 1940. His citation in the *London Gazette* read, 'Pilot Officer

O'Meara has displayed a very high degree of skill and devotion to duty in all operations against the enemy and has destroyed at least six enemy aircraft. His example and keenness have been outstanding.'

Flying Officer John Charles Dundas, of Cawthorne, was among others included in a list of awards announced by the Air Ministry. By October he had shot down eleven Nazi planes and had twice been shot down. John was shot down by German ace Helmut Wick, a pilot who had claimed fifty-six kills. John's brother Hugh was also a pilot during war who went on to become one of the youngest group captains in the RAF.

More and more land was allocated to support the 'Dig for Victory' campaign, and the council warned that flowers in public parks would be reduced to make way for growing vegetables. Gardens of unoccupied houses had also been requisitioned by the local authority. Reginald Dorman-Smith called for everyone to make use of any bit of land they could; even Locke Park was turned into a giant vegetable plot.

Sunday, 8 September 1940, witnessed one of the most impressive military spectacles ever seen in Barnsley. The No. 1 Barnsley Borough Battalion of the Home Guard marched with military precision in front of the Town Hall with 'eyes left' and Major Rideal taking the salute. Women hung out of the windows of the Barnsley Building Society, furiously waving Union Jacks in solidarity to the men below. Nine hundred men marched from St Mary's Parish Church, falling in on Churchfield, moving off via Sackville Street and Shambles Street to approach the saluting base from Market Hill. The parade was led by the Barnsley National Reserve and Gawber Bands. Major Rideal said the response of Home Guard recruitment had been 'encouraging on the whole, especially Carlton'.

This *Esprit de Corps* continued two weeks after the Home Guard impressed when the special constables, auxiliary fire service and the Barnsley squadron of the Air Defense Corps marched on the Town Hall, 400 men and women.

Barnsley WVS and the Home Guard helped more refugees as they streamed out of the capital and Hull, ending up in 'safe' areas such as Barnsley. In London, Barnsley's first female victim of enemy air action occurred with the death of Agnes Hawcroft. Agnes (47) and her sister Dorothy lived at Newholme, Pollitt Street, and both were transferred to London working for the unemployed assistance board. Agnes was schooled at Barnsley Central School while living at 122 Summer Lane, and later Barnsley Central College, finally finishing her education at the Barnsley School of Art. Leaving further education she worked at the GPO as a telephonist (switch board operator), then as a supervisor.

THE PHONEY WAR ENDS   101

Right: Connie
Howard (top left)
a Barnsley Land
Girl. Note the heavy
dungarees, typical
land girl 'uniform'.
(Barnsley Chronicle)

Below: Fruits
of labour after
Barnsley's Dig for
Victory campaign.
(Barnsley Chronicle)

Above and below: *These Land Army girls had just finished a month's training at Low Laithes Farm off the Barnsley–Wombwell Road. The trainees fared well, tending plough horses, driving tractors and looking after the stock. Working on a farm of 200 cattle the women woke at 5 am and finished at 5.30 pm.*

Barnsley Home Guard band marching in front of the ATS. (Barnsley Chronicle)

Soon after, Thomas Sellers, who owned a musical instrument business in west London, was killed in a bombing raid. He was born and raised in Barnsley and worked in his mum's grocery business on Cranbrook Street.

The public were reminded that in the event of Germans swarming up Eldon Street, roads must be kept clear for the movement of British troops and essential vehicles such as ARP, munitions and ambulances. The Germans issued their soldiers with maps of towns, including Barnsley, with key buildings identified. Recent bombing and air battles over England prompted a new warning to only attack parachutists who adopted a hostile attitude – the RAF contained Polish, Czech, French and Belgian airmen.

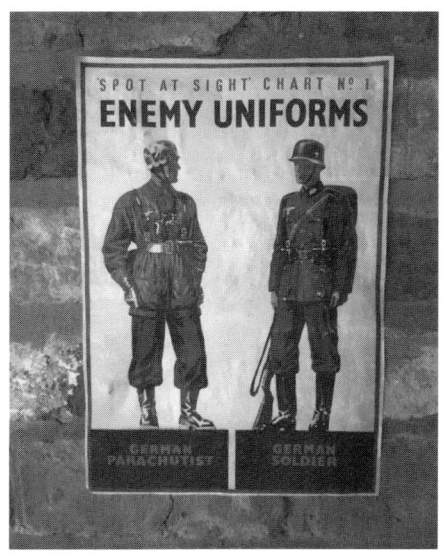

Barnsley had posters up advising people of the German uniforms to watch out for.

Issued by the Ministry of Information in co-operation with the War Office and the Ministry of Home Security

Beating the INVADER

A MESSAGE FROM THE PRIME MINISTER

IF invasion comes, everyone—young or old, men and women—will be eager to play their part worthily. By far the greater part of the country will not be immediately involved. Even along our coasts, the greater part will remain unaffected. But where the enemy lands, or tries to land, there will be most violent fighting. Not only will there be the battles when the enemy tries to come ashore, but afterwards there will fall upon his lodgments very heavy British counter-attacks, and all the time the lodgments will be under the heaviest attack by British bombers. The fewer civilians or non-combatants in these areas, the better—apart from essential workers who must remain. So if you are advised by the authorities to leave the place where you live, it is your duty to go elsewhere when you are told to leave. When the attack begins, it will be too late to go; and, unless you receive definite instructions to move, your duty will be to stay where you are. You will have ... into the safest place you can find, and stay ... til the battle is over. For all of you then ... order and the duty will be: "STAND FIRM".

This also applies to people inland if any considerable number of parachutists or air-borne troops are landed in their neighbourhood. Above all, they must not cumber the roads. Like their fellow-countrymen on the coasts, they must "STAND FIRM". The Home Guard, supported by strong mobile columns wherever the enemy's numbers require it, will immediately come to grips with the invaders, and there is little doubt will soon destroy them.

Throughout the rest of the country where there is no fighting going on and no close cannon fire or rifle fire can be heard, everyone will govern his conduct by the second great order and duty, namely, "CARRY ON". It may easily be some weeks before the invader has been totally destroyed, that is to say, killed or captured to the last man who has landed on our shores. Meanwhile, all work must be continued to the utmost, and no time lost.

The following notes have been prepar... everyone in rather more detail what to d... they should be carefully studied. Each man woman should think out a clear plan of pers... action in accordance with the general scheme.

Winston S. Churchill

STAND FIRM

1. What do I do if fighting breaks out in my neighbourhood?

Keep indoors or in your shelter until the battle is over. If you can have a trench ready in your garden or field, so much the better. You may want to use it for protection if your house is damaged. But if you are at work, or if you have special orders, carry on as long as possible and only take cover when danger approaches. If you are on your way to work, finish your journey if you can.

If you see an enemy tank, or a few enemy soldiers, do not assume that the enemy are in control of the area. What you have seen may be a party sent on in advance, or stragglers from the main body who can easily be rounded up.

Barnsley

Die Entfernungen nach den an den Ausfallstraßen angegebenen Orten betragen in Kilometer (von der rechten oberen Ecke im Sinne des Uhrzeigers fortschreitend):

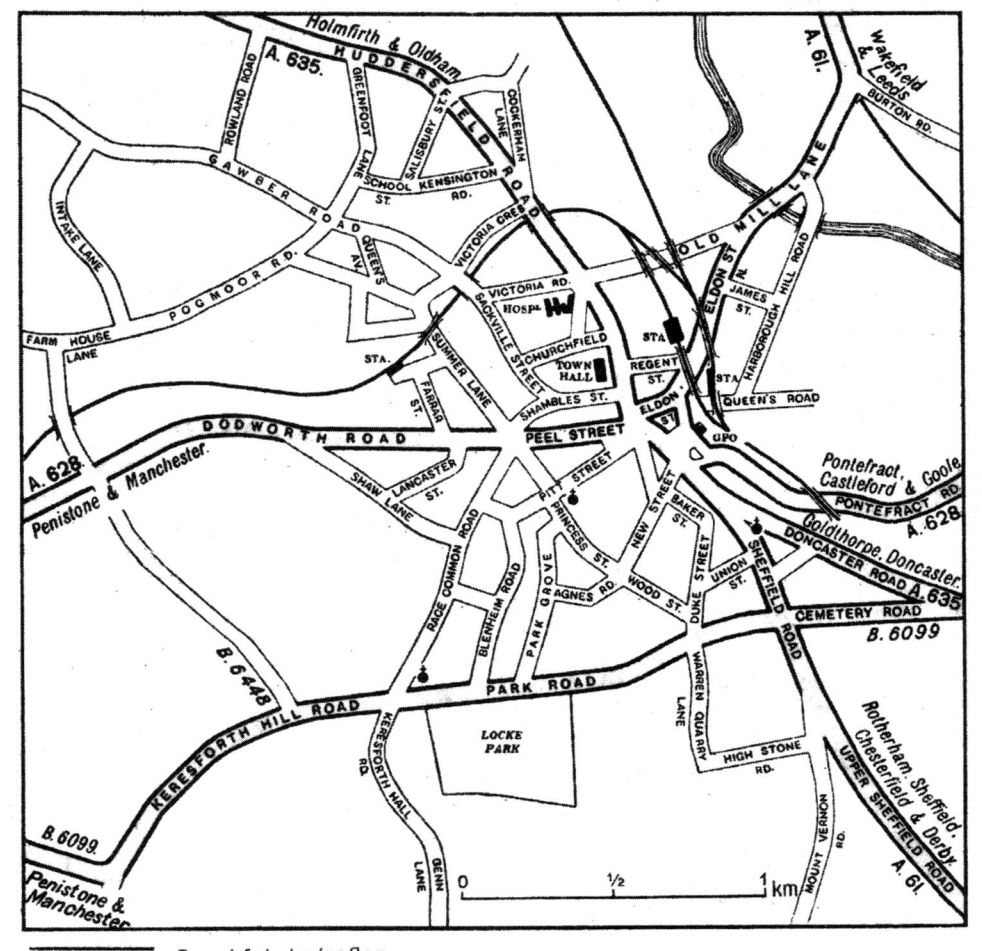

A 628:	Pontefract	20,9
	Castleford	25,7
	Goole	52,3
A 635:	Goldthorpe	11,3
	Doncaster	24,1
A 61:	Rotherham	17,7
	Sheffield	19,3
	Chesterfield	36,2
	Derby	73,2
B 6099:	Penistone	11,3
	Manchester	54,7
A 628:	Penistone	11,3
	Manchester	54,7
A 635:	Holmfirth	20,9
	Oldham	44,2
A 61:	Wakefield	16,1
	Leeds	29,0

═══ Durchfahrtsstraßen

German invasion town plan of Barnsley. (author's collection)

Barnsley 'kitchen front' week had been organised starting from 7 October 1940. That week if you walked on Eldon Street you could get free advice on wartime cookery and demonstrations, and at most senior schools in the borough more demonstrations and film shows were available. The *Barnsley Chronicle* and *South Yorkshire Times* both printed austere wartime recipes. Women of the WVS published a recipe book in aid of the mayor's Spitfire fund.

Because of the war the local Working Men's Club trip, the highlight of the children's year, had been cancelled. It was decided to compensate them with a half-pound box of chocolates, an apple, an orange and 6 shillings at Christmas. The club also gave to all its members' children between the ages of 5 and 14 a good pair of strong winter boots or shoes at a cost of £400. For Whitsuntide the committee treated the club to tea, sweets and ice-cream, entertainment by the Mirabelle Dancing Troupe and a picture show given by Mr F. Bentham.

Against the odds the Battle of Britain was won but the Blitz still had its iron grip on people's fears. The council proposed a new shelter near the Town Hall, and more domestic shelters were planned at various points in Barnsley.

The evacuation of children was in full flow by the autumn of 1940 following the German invasion of France and the beginning of the Blitz in September. How did those children feel? Some would find delight in their new homes, others would suffer from desperate homesickness and misery. 'Barnsley was Our Saviour' was the sentiment of Kath Parkin:

Kath Parkin before the war with her parents Mary and Alfred Holmes. (Memories of Barnsley)

The steam train wearily drew its last gasp as it pulled into Barnsley railway station. It was the end of a gruelling nine-hour journey for us: that is my mother, my sisters and myself. The journey had been interrupted several times. Wearily, we had been forced to alight from the train due to bombing raids on towns through which the train had travelled on its way from London. We got out of the train in Barnsley to a scene of pitch blackness and grime — and what on earth were people talking about? To us, from the South in 1942, three years before the declaration of peace in Europe, it could have been the moon on which we had landed. Everyone was speaking a foreign language, or so it seemed. And we didn't like what we saw. We thought we were going to a better place than we had left. Joyfully, when we became acclimatised to our new environment we realised we had. To begin with we couldn't come to terms with the quietness. No sound of throbbing aircraft. No sound of falling buildings and the breaking of glass. No craters in the ground and demolished houses, shops and churches. If only we could understand what people were saying to us, we would have known we were still in England. But, as far as we were concerned, we were utterly bemused evacuees. My mother, who had left her home town of Barnsley to work in London at 16, had decided to bring her young daughters back to her roots to escape the incessant bombing raids on Clapham Junction where we had been forced to move when our nice little house in Feltham had been 'requisitioned' by the RAF. She had been told on many occasions her children should be evacuated with other youngsters to Wales or some other quieter part of the country which the Germans didn't know about. But she had adamantly refused. 'Where they go, I go as well' she said.

After things got very bad, and we had spent many days hived up in an air-raid shelter in the back garden knee-deep in slimy flood water after violent thunderstorms, she decided 'enough was enough'. Next day, we packed our few possessions and set off. Back in 1942 London to Barnsley seemed a very long way and it must have taken her a great deal of courage to make the journey with her young children. Eventually, after living in cramped conditions in one room, we got our own house in Barnsley and we never returned to London.

Even though I was only a child, I will never forget the war years in London. Spending the night in the air-raid shelter and returning to find all our windows blown out. The wailing sirens of ambulances and fire engines, the dreadful misery and deprivation. Barnsley was our saviour and we shall always be thankful for that. And for the fact we were still alive and well to celebrate VE Day here.

Kath worked for the *Barnsley Chronicle* for many years after the war and her story was published in the spring 2008 edition of *Barnsley Memories*.

During this intake of evacuees the Old Rectory and Obelisk House, among others, were used for billeting. Weekly allowances for householders who billeted were:

each single adult, 21/0d
each pair of adults, 35/0d
each child aged 14 to 17, 10/6d
each child under 14, 8/6d

Armistice Day was observed in Barnsley with two minutes' silence and the laying of wreaths on local memorials. On a lighter note the grand opening of a new

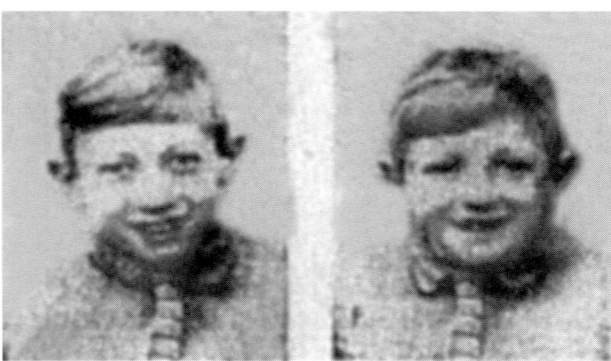

Above and left: London evacuees Roy and Raymond Greasley, well-known London entertainers who had been evacuated to London to live with relatives; the other image is of the lads in the 1960s.

'super' cinema in Royston called ACE thrilled audiences with its heavy piled carpets, luxurious push-up seats for 750 people, and ample leg room. The famous Western Electric Mirrophonic sound system provided cutting-edge sound. To book seats and enjoy this 'amazing cinema experience' you had to call the manager Mr Silverwood on Carlton Lane. Captain Hallam formally opened the cinema, that only took six months to build. *Green Hell* with Douglas Fairbanks and *Devil on Wheels* starring Ann Sheridan were some of the first films shown, and the cinema also kept people up to date with the latest war news from Universal News Service.

In France, Barnsley men were still busy clocking up awards and medals. Private Albert Ibbotson (22) eldest son of Albert Ibbotson, High Street, Penistone, was awarded the coveted French honour, Croix de Guerre. William Shaw of Cromwell Street, Thurnscoe, was also presented with a Croix de Guerre by President de Gaulle at the Arc de Triomphe for his actions in ambushing a group of German soldiers who were about to attack.

Three brothers who were evacuees from Carshalton, Surrey. They were billeted at Ashton House, Carlton Road, and then moved to 25 Carlton Road to stay with a widow, Mrs Emma Boyd, who died in 1956. Emma was mother to four grown up children of her own. (Memories of Barnsley)

Nine weeks after winning the DFM for 'great courage in attacks against the enemy,' George Cecil 'Grumpy' Unwin of Bolton-upon-Dearne was awarded a bar to his medal. During the Battle of Britain, stationed in No. 12 Group, he was credited with fourteen enemy aircraft shot down by the end of 1940. On 15 September Unwin claimed three Bf 109s destroyed (Luftwaffe records indicate they were from JG 77) and on the 18th he added a Bf 110 to his score as his 11th victory. On the 27th he destroyed a Bf 109- Wrk Nr 6162 of JG 52, and on 5 November scored a kill against a JG 51 Bf 109- Wrk Nr 4846. Unwin had now destroyed eight 109s. On 5 November he shot down his final personal victory, a Bf 110 over the English Channel. In that engagement he was attacked by Hauptmann Gerhard Schöpfel of JG 26 who claimed Unwin as one of

Flight Sergeant 'Grumpy' Unwin, right, confers with Squadron Leader 'Sandy' Lane, centre, at RAF Fowlmere, September 1940. 'Grumpy' of Bolton-upon-Dearne was credited with fourteen enemy aircraft shot down by the end of 1940.

two kills, but Unwin was not shot down. At the end of 1940 he was rested and sent as an instructor to No. 2 Central Flying School, Cranwell.

Bolton-upon-Dearne was breeding RAF heros. Another airman to gain distinction was Sergeant Wilfred Scarrott who won the DFM. He was the wireless operator/air gunner on a photo reconnaissance mission over France when his aircraft was attacked from astern by two ME 109s. In the first burst of fire Wilf was wounded in the face and his gun-sight was shot away. Despite his injury he returned a long burst sending one of the 109s to a watery grave.

Sheffield was next in Hitler's sights. The prime target was supposed to be the River Don Works, which manufactured crankshafts and other components for Spitfires and Hurricanes, but worst hit was the city centre along with Sharrow, Nether Edge, Heeley, Pitsmoor, Broomhill, Millhouses, Meersbrook, and Woodseats. People who lived on Ecclesall Road were victims of surplus bombs and incendiaries. Contemporary German maps show the factories marked as secondary targets; primary targets appeared to be hospitals, schools and railways, suggesting the Sheffield Blitz was mostly a terror raid designed to bomb the population into submission. Barrage balloons were organised from Norton aerodrome to discourage low-flying enemy aircraft. They could be clearly seen from Barnsley. A Leyland vehicle was rushed into Sheffield from Barnsley on 12 December 1940, then on the 13th at 12.42 am Sheffield Police Fire Brigade requested assistance from other neighbouring Fire Brigades. In response Manchester and Nottingham sent ten pumps each, Bradford sent six, Barnsley four, Doncaster, Wakefield, Halifax, and Huddersfield sent three each, and Rotherham, Wombwell, Leeds and York each sent two. Manned pumps also arrived from Mexborough, Wortley, Hoyland, Kiveton Park, Thorne, Wath, Cudworth, Pudsey, Morley, Spenborough, Pontefract, Shipley, Bingley, Keighley, Brighouse, Elland, Holmfirth, Castleford, Mirfield and Ossett. Outside help totalled 70 pumps and 522 men. Some of the outside pumps had difficulty getting into the city and had to be guided round bomb craters by men of Sheffield Transport Department. They and the local services were hampered by water freezing under their feet and on their clothes.

German propaganda relished the moment in a radio broadcast:

During the night of December 12-13 Sheffield, the centre of British heavy industry, was attacked for the first time by strong German bomber formations. Favourable weather and visibility enabled the crews to find their targets and

Sheffield Blitz – you can clearly see the bombs dropped on the city were concentrated on the city centre and not on outlying industrial areas such as Meadowhall or Attercliffe.

112 BARNSLEY AT WAR 1939–45

Above: The historic Leyland vehicle was rushed into the Steel City from Barnsley on 12 December 1940, the first night of the Sheffield Blitz (thank you to National Emergency Services Museum, Old Police/ Fire Station, West Bar, Sheffield).

Left: Manning the defences of Sheffield are some of the Barnsley Territorials Anti-Aircraft Battery.

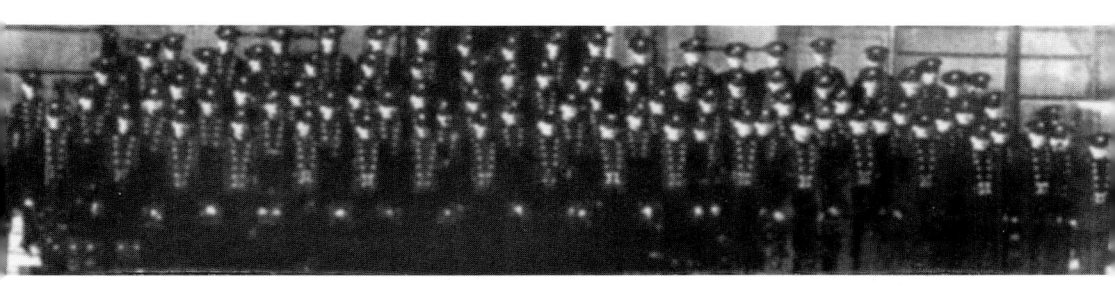

Barnsley's 200-strong Auxiliary Fire Service. Some of these men would have seen service in the Sheffield and Manchester Blitz.

clearly to ascertain the effects of their attack. According to all reports the effects of the attack were similar to those of Coventry...

On the Sunday night the raiders were met with an astonishingly heavy AA barrage, including guns from Barnsley and Penistone. Residents at Stocksbridge would have seen the bombs dropping near Heights Farm where Stan Crossland, his wife and three children had a lucky escape when bombs dropped just 20 yards away from where they were sleeping. Fires could be seen from Dodworth, Pogmoor and the top of Worsbrough Common.

That same night a request was sent to Dodworth for ARP services to stand by in case they were required to proceed to a neighbouring town to give help in a raid there. A further request was made for them to obtain supplies of rations to take with them should they be required. On Sunday night all the shops were closed so the wardens organised a small house-to-house collection; this turned into a competition as one householder was not to be outdone by the other. Finally, 271 loaves of bread were collected from the kind-hearted people of Dodworth, despite their own food shortages.

At the request of Mr English, local organiser at Dodworth, the loaves were given and gratefully received by the people of Sheffield. The following day a further collection was made of cash, bread, tea, soup, salmon, beans and all sorts of other groceries. Mr Maltas, senior warden for Dodworth, was instrumental in organising relief for the Sheffielders.

The council of Yorkshire Mineworkers Association at Barnsley donated £1,500 to the city's distress fund, and a furniture van loaded with supplies for our shell-shocked neighbours was sent over. Barnsley had already sent a mobile food canteen to London (two in total, one later in the war) and supplies to Coventry and Birmingham before the Sheffield Blitz. Hoyland also sent over AFS volunteers to support.

Mr Fred Sargeant, a reserve fireman, playing darts with his fellow fighters. (photo courtesy of Roundhouse Community Partnership)

Over the Pennines in Manchester sixteen members of the Barnsley AFS were drafted for duty during their blitz. A brave act was reported by a Mr Lonsdale of the AFS. He was returning to the fire station with a colleague when a policeman called him over to assist in some rescue work. After removing a large quantity of debris, they succeeded in making a hole to the cellars of the smouldering, demolished building, giving scant regard for their own safety. With the cellars on the point of collapse, Lonsdale entered and rescued the three scared occupants who were clinging to life. Remarkably after receiving a strong stimulant (probably whisky) he continued with firefighting duty the rest of the night. A Barnsley hero!

George Adams, an old Barnsley soldier who served in the Boer War and a sergeant with one of the Barnsley battalions in the Great War, moved to Manchester in 1937. George, 64, was a senior warden for the Manchester ARP and was on duty at his post near the cathedral at the time of the Blitz. Bombs hit nearby injuring George who died a few days later. His daughter, Mrs Cadman, who lived at 'Crossways', Upper Dodworth Road, attended his funeral at Ardsley cemetery. Among the floral tributes was a wreath from the Manchester City ARP service.

Gallant efforts by the Royston Rescue Service were acknowledged by the chairman of the Emergency Committee. Under the leadership of the Royston council surveyor, Mr H. Clarke, the men, although it was Christmas Eve, were happy to help the unfortunate Mancs.

In Liverpool an entire Ward Green family was wiped out by a single bomb at their home. The house, on Hornby Place, a small street off Hornby Road near the prison, was home to George Henry Simm, his wife Phyllis and their two children, Keitha, 6, and Gary, 2. Phyllis survived the initial blast but later succumbed to her injuries and died at Walton Hospital. The others died beneath the debris, their charred bodies being recovered later. George was a warder at Walton Gaol, which itself was bombed earlier in the year killing twenty-two inmates. On that December night he had just gone to bed in the cellar after organising a Christmas event for his colleagues. The bomb killed him instantly. George married Phyllis Rennison in 1932 at St Luke's Church, Worsbrough Common. Before the war he had served six years in the Royal Artillery and before that worked at Barrow Colliery.

George and Phyllis Simm with their son Gary. All the family including their other child Keitha died in the Liverpool Blitz. (thank you to Collette Rooke)

In Coventry, Harold Bates, formerly of High Street, Worsbrough Dale, was killed while on fire-watch duty. He had worked at the Yorkshire Traction Depot and before that Wombwell Main Colliery before moving to Coventry to start a new life.

Events in Sheffield and over the Pennines brought home the dangers of bombs and particularly the dangers of incendiary devices. Sand was ordered and distributed accordingly, enough for every house.

For the first time in twenty-two years women delivered the post in Barnsley, 140 of them. They had last done so in the Great War for the Christmas rush. Back in those days letters were delivered everyday over the Christmas period including Christmas Day and Boxing Day.

January to June 1941

In North Africa, Tobruk was targeted by the Allied army after Australian troops captured Italian-held Bardia and 45,000 Italian prisoners were taken. Tobruk, the next mark, was 70 miles away and on 7 January an Allied force took the airport. That encouraging news stimulated the home front.

By January Penistone had 204 persons serving with the forces. Three were PoWs: Kenneth Fowler, Harold Moorehouse and Spencer Stanley. Included in the 204 are Mrs Bakewell, Miss Mary Crownshaw, Mary Jones and Miss Betty Keen, all engaged in nursing of some sort.

Royston's proudest boy in January was Philip Julian Griffiths who received a signed copy of Winston Churchill's *My Early Life*. Philip had earlier received a signed autograph book of Churchill's War Cabinet which was given to him via his grandfather George, who was MP for the Hemsworth division. A few days later George was in the smoke room at the House and told Mr Churchill how delighted Philip was with the autographs. Smiling, the Prime Minister said, 'When is his Birthday? Write his name down for me.' George wrote down the date and gave it to Churchill who put it into his waistcoat pocket. On Philip's birthday a bulky parcel, stamped First Lord of the Treasury, arrived containing an autographed copy of the book. A few years later the Griffiths family moved away from Barnsley and Philip's daughter Jane offered the books at auction asking that the proceeds go for the benefit of young people in Royston. The books were sold by Christie's for £2,400 in 2007.

Royston's proudest man was James Arthur Allanach of Hollycroft Avenue, who won the coveted Knightian Medal for the best cultivated garden in Great Britain. The medal, part of the Dig for Victory campaign, was presented by the Royal Horticultural Society. Born in 1893, he was president of the Royston Royal British Legion Sports Club, secretary for the Royston Land Fertility Scheme, secretary of the Royston Benevolent Fund, secretary for the Horticultural Society and secretary for the Royston Carnival Flower and Vegetable Show. He was married to Mary Sheldon and died in 1984.

Plans for Barnsley War Weapons Week were in full swing by the end of January. The event was to raise £500,000, the cost of a destroyer.

'Lend to Win' was the slogan. The purchase of National War Bonds, Defense Bonds, Savings Bonds, Savings Certificates and Post Office and York County Savings Bank deposits all counted to the final tally. A large sales indicator was to be erected on top of Market Hill recording progress.

Later in the war a tank was spotted in Burma by Sergeant James Cook whose wife and 6-year-old son lived at Vernon Way, Gawber Road. James saw the tank racing through the desert with 'Barnsley' painted on the side. After a few enquiries it transpired it was built by money raised from War Weapons Week.

A Messerschmitt 109 was on view on a site near the Town Hall and a purchase of five savings stamps would allow the buyer to sit in the pilot's seat of the German, single seat fighter.

THE PHONEY WAR ENDS 117

Barnsley War Weapons week; all the towns and villages in the district exceeded their targets.

A total of £1,003,449 8s. 7d. was raised – over twice the amount of the original aim of half a million pounds, enough to build a sister ship.

Recruiting continued for the regular armed services and all aspects of home protection with most Barnsley districts boasting at least a one Home Guard Company, AFS units, Nursing Reserve, St Johns Ambulance, Red Cross, Special Police etc.

London had the Krays, Chicago entertained Al Capone and in 1941 Barnsley was terrorised by the 'Redhill Gang'. Working out of a hut the gang devised their plans to steal from air raid shelters. Working under cover of darkness, the nine-strong gang from Kendray terrorised residents by wearing masks with slits for their eyes and a hole for their nose, identifying themselves with the letter 'R' on each side of their mask and on a badge. The boys paid the 15-year-old leader a penny a week for membership. Assembled in their den they made their audacious plans and surreptitiously puffed on cigarettes. The Fagin-style leader sometimes gave them sweets. Inspired by what they had seen at the cinema the boys would sit in the shed until late in the evening roasting potatoes. Eviction from this secret society would happen if the boys created trouble or didn't pay their subs. Arriving on duty one day, a policeman was told that lamps had been stolen from some of the shelters. After some detective work he found his way to a hut at the back of a boy's home. Breaking down the door the policeman

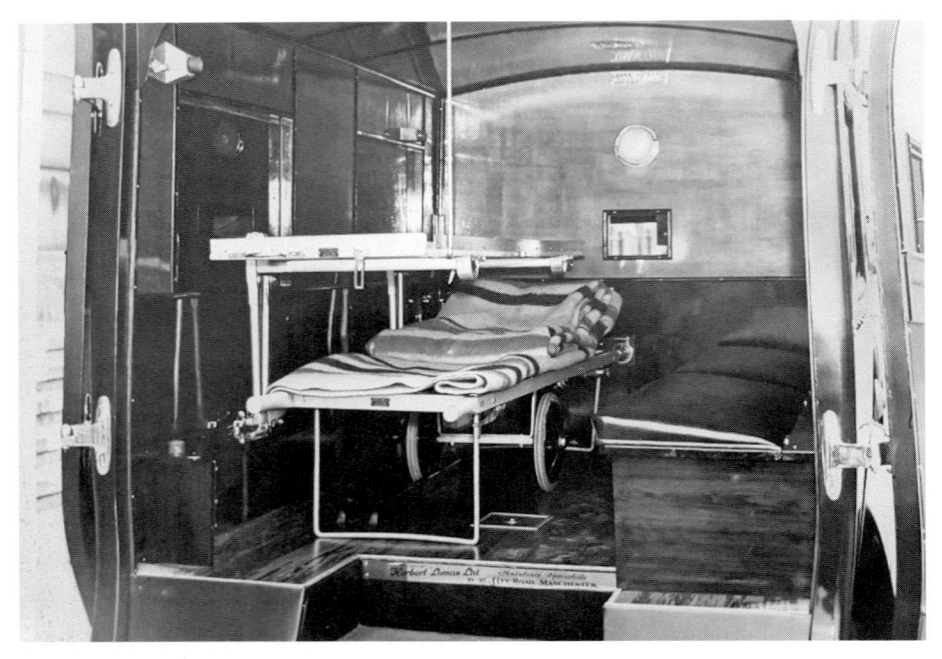

Barnsley Auxiliary Ambulance built by Herbert Lomas of Manchester. (Barnsley Chronicle)

found various stolen articles including the lamps. The boys were fined, ordered to disband the gang and attend Sunday school.

A more sinister gang made up of six youths from the borough were committed for trial at Leeds Assizes by the Barnsley County Borough magistrates. They were George Goodman (22), Walter Nuttall (18), William Lawrence (17), Thomas Morley (19), Stanley Houghton (17) and an unnamed 16-year-old, all on charges of assaults and robbery. Terrorising locals with knuckle dusters these lads seemingly robbed at will. After robbing the first victim, Maurice Sheridan, of £4, the gang then relieved Alan Rennison of £3. They then proceeded to attack five other people in five various parts of the town under cover of the blackout. Three of the five were attacked so fiercely that they fell to the ground bleeding and were kicked into insensibility before being stripped of their valuables. All were tried and sentenced.

Public optimism had risen since the recent Allied victories in Libya, easing the fears of invasion. Captain Harry Barker, who was living at Regent Gardens, Huddersfield Road, with his wife who was a corporal with the ATS, had recently taken part in the British advances in Italy's North African colony. Barker described conditions of sweltering heat, dusty and oily, with enemy shells falling close to his 25-ton Matilda tank and shrapnel rattling and pinging off the hull. They lived in the desert between actions under tarpaulins rigged against the side of the tank. He also told of a stay in a captured Italian camp. Food was not plentiful but sufficient, he said, and they cooked on petrol cookers. Harry was commissioned into the Royal Tank Regiment two years before the war and was promoted to captain in Christmas 1940.

Winter blackouts times were receding, and Easter was firmly in the chocolate-needy minds of children of the borough.

Barnsley's landscape changed in April when iron railings were targeted for the government's metal campaign. Railings belonging to churches, houses large and small, council estates and business premises were removed, leaving only iron stumps protruding above low walls. Hundreds of miles of railings vanished from the streets of Barnsley. Iron railings from the top of Churchfield had been sacrificed by the council to set the example; workmen using an acetylene burning plant severed the iron rails from the lower part of the wall. There was a further drive for railing metal in January 1942.

No structure was safe from the sandbags – note the iron railings at the front; these were removed later in the war. (Daily Mail)

Iceland was occupied by the British in the war to deny it to Germany. Lance Corporal Tom Dook of the King's Own was one of many men from Barnsley who were charged defending the island. Tom had to adapt quickly to the cold climate.

Norman Ellis from Dodworth was on leave and not looking forward to his new assignment in Iceland. After being issued with his Arctic kit, Norman boarded the troopship SS *Orduna*, and then sailed with two escorting destroyers towards Iceland. The seas were rough, the food was 'poor', and Norman suffered from sea sickness and headaches, and was unable to keep down his rations. Disembarking at Reykjavik, Norman also remarked on the cold. The men were given 10 Kroner to spend in the capital and sixty cigarettes. After a day of rest Norman and his group were ordered on a route march wearing

Silkstone Home Guard. (courtesy of Paul Wilkinson)

winter fatigues. During that month Norman climbed a 5,000 foot glacier in the north of the country, with Major Scott, the Arctic explorer in charge of mountaineering. He also slept in a wind-proof tent, skied and played football. Norman's diary is available to view at the archives in Barnsley Town Hall, including photos of his adventures; it is well worth a visit.

Shorter blackout times were announced by the government when the clocks were put forward by one hour at the beginning of May.

On a May morning in 1941, Barnsley 'C' Company had the objective of capturing Dodworth Church from 2 and 3 Platoons of the Silkstone and Dodworth Home Guard. The whole of 'C' company were either captured or destroyed while the defenders suffered the loss of two outposts and about twenty-five men. But Dodworth Church was safe, for now!

In the spring of 1941, to combat the severity of rationing, the government set up what were known as British Restaurants. They were to sell basic meals at reasonable prices, off-ration. They were sited to be in easy reach of most families.

THE PHONEY WAR ENDS 121

County Borough of Barnsley
British Restaurant
PUBLIC HALL

BARNSLEY'S FIRST BRITISH RESTAURANT, in the Public Hall, under the auspices of the War Emergency Committee, will be OFFICIALLY OPENED on WEDNESDAY NEXT, the 12th November, 1941, at 11.45 a.m.

The Opening Ceremony will be performed by the Chairman of the Social Welfare Committee (Mr. Councillor Mason, J.P.).

Immediately after the opening ceremony meals will be available for the public on the premises at the following prices, approved by the Ministry of Food, viz.:—

Meat & Vegetables	**- 6d.**
Meat & Vegetables (for children)	**- 4d.**
Soup	- 1d.
Sweet	- 2d.
Cup of Tea	- 1d.
Bread	– Free

Town Hall,
BARNSLEY.

A. E. GILFILLAN,
Town Clerk.

Left and below: One of Barnsley's civic restaurants at the top floor of the Civic Hall. (Barnsley Chronicle)

The first one in Barnsley was opened in Worsbrough and known as 'The Dale'. It was established at the Old Keel Inn, Worsbrough Dale, with seating for forty-eight people. Meals could either be taken away or eaten at the Keel. Soup was a penny; meat and two veg, sixpence; and sweet pudding, tuppence. The restaurants, run by the ever willing WVS, served quality and filling food. Lundwood followed in November and the third, in March 1942, at the Barnsley Society of the New Church in Parker Street. St Luke's School, Worsbrough Common, hosted the fourth and a fifth one was established at Stairfoot. Locke Park hosted another in April 1943. To boost the vitamin intake of children, the Ministry of Health made sure that every child received daily milk, cod liver oil and orange juice, and published 'Food Facts' in newspapers.

May 1941 saw the peak of the blitzing of Hull. Hull suffered some of the country's most devastating attacks during the war. As with Manchester and Liverpool, Barnsley rushed to the aid of the East Coast town, this time not with the AFS but with forty builders. Members of the party, who were all volunteers, had been recruited from the employees of Vernon Dunk Ltd., H. Field and Son and Wm. Johnson and Sons.

Another notable event in May was the sinking of HMS *Hood* by the *Bismarck* during The Battle of the Denmark Strait. When the *Bismarck* and the *Prinz Eugen* sailed for the Atlantic in May 1941, the *Hood* and the battleship *Prince of Wales* were sent out in pursuit to prevent them breaking into the Atlantic where they could attack Allied convoys.

Mrs Chivers of Racecommon Road feared the worst when the *Hood* went down because on board was her husband Chief Petty Officer Arthur Chivers who worked in the engine room. Arthur was a Navy veteran who had served aboard HM ships *Glasgow* and *Dorsetshire*. When the magazine of the *Hood* was hit, an enormous explosion ripped through the ship, killing Arthur.

Back in town the new fashion for women was the Jacoll hat at 5/11 available from the Co-operative drapery department. But clothing became scarce as clothes rationing began on 1 June 1941. Clothes rationing ended on 15 March 1949. The government issued a clothing book with coloured coupons. Every item of clothing was given a value in coupons. To buy clothes people handed over their clothing book to the shopkeeper who cut out one of the coupons. People used army blankets and parachute silk to meet their fashion needs. To save fabric, men's trousers were made without turnups and women's skirts were shortened and cut straight with minimal trimmings.

A memorial service was held on Sunday, 29 June, in acknowledgment of the local men, women and children from Barnsley who had died. A parade of ex-service men, Home Guard battalions, Civil Defense services and other organisations were invited to the event at Locke Park.

Rumours circulated around town that the famous butcher family of Albert Hirst was using horse meat in his products. Executors of Albert's estate issued a warning in the *Chronicle*, threatening legal proceedings against anyone making such claims. This was a common accusation made against butchers in many towns during the war.

David (Dai) Grenfell who was the Minister of Mines in 1941 appealed to the miners of Barnsley to give every ounce of their energy and every possible minute of their time to producing as much coal as possible. He laid down a five-point plan to accelerate the industry. Management was encouraged to concentrate on maximum production, the eradication of absenteeism, and more men must be taken on, especially those with previous experience of the industry.

On a hot Friday in late June, 5-year-old Iris Lenton was paddling at the junction of the rivers Dearne and Dove with her brother Philip and some other friends. Philip watched his sister come out of the water and start putting on her socks and shoes, but he became distracted by watching other boys swimming and did not notice Iris go back into the water. Later he saw her missing from the bank and, scanning the water, he saw Iris's flapping little hand just above the water. John Clarke, a haulage hand from Ings Road, was swimming a couple of hundred yards away when a panic stricken little boy on a bicycle told him a little girl was drowning. About four minutes went by before he found Iris, but when John got the girl out she had died.

Another boy bathing that day was John Butterworth of Great Houghton. He was watching boys and girls paddling when he noticed a little girl walk out of the Dove into the Dearne and then disappear as though she had fallen into a mud hole. He desperately shouted to Eileen Woodcock to get Iris out. Eileen saw several little girls wandering into the river. Knowing it was deep in parts, she shouted for them to get back and ran to stop them going further. Eileen managed to reach 3-year-old Maureen Eyre and Joan Rollins aged 9. She got the two girls back to the safety of the Dove but failed to rescue Iris. Iris's heartbroken mother Marion stoutly remarked, 'I think they tried to do their best, there is always someone paddling there.' Iris's father was serving as a soldier in the army.

July to December 1941

As Russia was facing up to the might of the *Wehrmacht*, in Barnsley there was a memorial service in Locke Park to remember the men of the town who made the supreme sacrifice in the Somme offensive of July 1916. It gave the townsfolk

The Somme Parade, 29 June 1941. (Barnsley Chronicle)

the opportunity to see the Home Guard and Civil Defense services in drill action, a sight of which Barnsley could be proud. The women's ATS was praised for a well-organised and successful demonstration. The memorial service was followed by a recruiting campaign encouraged by the band of the ITC York and Lancaster Regiment.

A few days later the girls of the ATS made a good impression when they visited Barnsley on the 4 July 1941. Walking past the Royal Hotel, eyes left, they swung along Market Hill in their neat khaki uniforms, with shoulders thrown back, arms swinging and rank by rank in step. In front of the women was again the band of the ITC York and Lancaster Regiment under the direction of Mr H. Ivimey. Taking the salute was Mayor Walton. The contingent was in town to aid a recruiting drive for the women's services.

Barnsley Fire Brigade acquired itself a new Leyland 45-hp with the registration plate HE 9686. The new engine was fitted with an enclosed cab for the driver and three men, with four men just behind them, and two on the back. It had a searchlight with tripod and detachable cable, a first aid reel and extension ladders. Pumps at the rear were powerful enough to deliver 800 gallons per minute. The brigade already had a similar Leyland that was eight years older, a Chrysler car with

Members of the Barnsley ATS with a donated wireless set. (Barnsley Chronicle)

trailer pump and hose and a 1920 model fire engine. Superintendent W. Heyhurst had fifteen full-time and twenty-two part-time firefighters under his charge at the Barnsley station.

Revenge for the *Hood* was top of the Admiralty's priority. Now the *Bismarck*, with her crew of 2,200, was a sitting duck for the Royal Navy in the Atlantic, with her steering jammed and her speed reduced by torpedo attacks. Sub-Lieutenant Leslie Bailey of Pogmoor had a hand in the thrilling aerial hunt for the mighty German battleship and pride of the *Kriegsmarine*. He had just celebrated his 19th birthday in May, and up to then was thought to be the youngest qualified observer and wireless telegraphist in the British Navy. Leslie was with the aircraft carrier *Victorious* and in a contemporary interview which avoided the censors, Leslie gave this account:

Sub-Lieutenant Leslie Bailey of Pogmoor had a hand in the thrilling aerial hunt for the Bismarck.

Ablaze and with vast plumes of smoke rising from it, the Bismarck *takes hit after hit from British ships and the Fairey Swordfish torpedo planes.*

> In dirty weather we went on a reconnaissance mission in his Swordfish [SFx.631 piloted by Lieutenant N.G. MacLean] at 10 pm. As soon as we could we formed up and set off on a course of 225 degrees and about an hour later the faster Fulmars [Royal Navy fighters] overtook us making our way to the German ship at about 80–85 knots.
>
> At 11:30 pm contact was made through a gap in the cloud but we soon lost sight again. We reduced altitude and were directed towards the Bismarck by HMS Norfolk who was shadowing the German ship.
>
> We got separated and when we finally started our run we were met with a most vigorous barrage at midnight; we had planned to attack starboard but decided at the last minute to attack the port side. As we turned away we sprayed the ship with bullets as a final bon-voyage.

Cinema goers in the town would have seen Leslie on board the *Victorious* after the battle with three of his fellow officers.

Morale improved when Hitler attacked Russia, followed by the signing of the Anglo-Russian agreement. Occupying the Germans in the east could only be good news for the Allies. Nevertheless Barnsley continued their defensive preparations for the town. Looking down from the high plateau between Lundwood and the main railway line running through Cudworth towards the Common and near the Lundwood Smallpox Hospital, the part-time soldiers gathered with regular troops commanded by Colonel Neill, the zone commander. Standing in front of a microphone the colonel issued orders. The Home Guard were to be the 'Germans' with the regulars holding the line on the bracken-covered ground. The paratroopers had grounded on Cudworth Common astride the railway

THE PHONEY WAR ENDS 127

Colonel Neill, zone commander, addressing members of the Home Guard following exercises with regular troops at Lundwood.

line to the strength of one company with a few light tanks. The Home Guard enemy concentrated under cover of the embankment and advanced towards the Barnsley–Pontefract Road. On high ground to the north and from down the hill to the west the enemy stealthily crept forward. Fire was withheld until they were nearby and then machine gun and rifle fire echoed out towards the borough. After the attack, a victory for the regulars, Colonel Neill demonstrated a trench mortar to the Home Guard.

A peculiar drill was announced by the War Emergency Committee on 16 August with the plan to release, by means of generators, war gas in the vicinity of Cheapside and the Kendray housing estate. The notice encouraged people to be vigilant and carry their gas masks always. If someone was unfortunate to get in the gas cloud with defective masks they would not have been comforted by the warning of a 'temporary but most intense discomfort and burning of the eyes'. If symptoms persisted then the affected had to visit their nearest ARP first aid post, where trained personnel would be available to give medical attention. The exercise was cancelled at the last minute, but it did take place in September.

Feast Week, which was known that year as 'stay at home Feast Week', hosted demonstrations in August and September including a mock battle involving a tank trap. Valentine and Matilda tanks rolled into town, and Mayor Walton hitched a ride on one. Playing the band and heading the procession was the Home Guard. Most collieries observed Feast Week that year so there was no shortage of spectators. A comprehensive tour of the town was organised over three days.

128   BARNSLEY AT WAR 1939–45

Above and below: The men of the Royal Tank Corps found the Mayor and the Home Guard waiting to escort them from Stairfoot during Feast Week. (Barnsley Chronicle)

With many Barnsley men PoWs somewhere in Europe, Barnsley formed a relatives' association to 'extend a certain amount of cheer and comfort to prisoners of war'. Profiles of PoWs were being printed in the *Chronicle* weekly. In March 1943, Barnsley held a Rally Week to support prisoners overseas.

Barnsley man First Class Stoker James Kenneth Walton was eyewitness to the pivotal meeting of Winston Churchill and Franklin D. Roosevelt on board HMS *Prince of Wales* in August of 1941. It was later known as the Atlantic Conference. He wrote:

You will have heard by now the reason I have not written before. We have had the Premier and other distinguished personages including heads of the fighting forces on board... The PM is exactly like his photos, as they do not flatter him one bit – the determined look on his face as if he felt ready to take a bite out of Hitler's leg. Also, I saw the President of the United States in company with Mr Churchill. We had a church service aboard on the Sunday in lovely weather and I understand they are including a scene in a newsreel. The singing was like one big choir raising their voices to heaven... the meeting will be an occasion to remember and talk about, God willing, long after Hitler and his Nazi creed have gone.

James Kenneth was the son of the Mayor, James Walton. He did not survive the war but died on board the *Prince of Wales* on 10 December 1941.

Back home, as part of the government's plan to strengthen the organisation of fire prevention, the Commissioner for the North Eastern Region announced areas where fire watching duties would be compulsory. Barnsley was one of the areas affected so dates were set for registration for men between 18 and 30.

Fire watching was compulsory but some did not take it seriously: George Watson, James Darn and Harry Lyons all pled guilty to breaches of the Fire Prevention Order. Mr Booth prosecuting said that these men were required to fire watch at their place of work in Penistone. They were told by their foreman and by the pay clerk. Darn refused to come on duty and the other two blamed a lively Feast Week. At these works no-one was required to do more than nine hours of fire duty in a month. The defendants were each fined 20 shillings.

The family of Martin Burke would have been delighted to hear him on the radio speaking from Cairo. He was one of a few men selected to send Christmas greetings home to his family. His wife and four children tuned in to the BBC to hear their father's voice. It was the first time they had heard from Martin since his last letter six weeks previously.

November's Poppy Day appeal was in full swing with tributes planned throughout the borough. The new mayor, Alderman Reverend D. Allott, reminded citizens of the continuing need to support the war effort.

Government training centres for women were starting to open in the borough. The war was being fought in the factories in the town and women who were starting work had to learn their crafts. Barnsley was one of thirty-five training centres in the country, where hairdressers, shop assistants and even domestic servants learned their trades. On entering the machine shop you would have been confronted with rows and rows of machines. The longest course was twenty-six weeks and the women were trained in all aspects of machine operating including bench fitting and sheet metal working. The machine operating classes were divided into sections. The aptitude of any trainee was quickly identified and they would be drafted into a specialised section

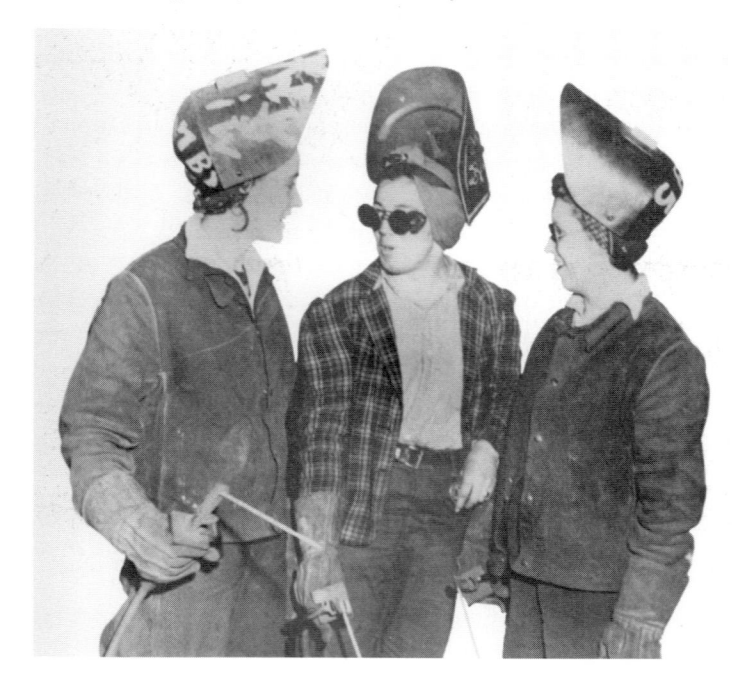

Martin Burke, who spoke to his wife and family from Cairo, something today we all take for granted.

Women metal workers during the war.

such as a capstan lathe or tool room operative. One of these centres was used by Firth-Vickers to make aero parts at Measborough Dike, Doncaster Road, then after the war was used and owned by Slazenger's. Other centres that were used for war work included Beatson Clark & Co, Downings Ltd who made Anderson Shelters, Qualter Hall & Co who manufactured parts for the Mulberry Harbour used on D-Day, Hickson, Lloyd and King at Redbrook who made heavy cotton goods, and Fox's at Stocksbridge.

Edith Horn (21) of Station Road, Ryhill, Nancy Watson (21) of Charles Street, Worsbrough Bridge, and Winifred Hawcroft (22) of 14 Honeywell Street, Barnsley, worked in the factories. One said that it was 'quite interesting work', 'conditions were good', 'people were sociable and always willing to help', 'her lodgings were comfortable, and she had plenty to eat; the recreational facilities were also good.' Fancy clothing was out; the working women wore trousers or dungarees with their hair tied up in a scarf, often done up in a head square turban – a distinctive wartime look.

ICI in Huddersfield was employing women in their factory. A bus picked them up under Stairfoot Bridge at 6.30 am and would return at 6 pm. Molly Casey

Above left: Women were drafted into job roles that became extinct after the Great War.

Above right: A beautiful glass window on display at Eden Camp near Malton in North Yorkshire. The camp was home to Italian and German PoWs.

Emma Thompson meeting the Princess Royal on her visit to the tank factory at Monk Bretton. (Memories of Barnsley)

(née Thompson) tells of her mother's experience working at ICI. 'In the evenings, especially when it became warm from the coal fire, her clothes would start to change colour, especially her underwear...sometimes yellow and more often red.' Molly's mum started to look ill, losing weight and having a terrible cough. She goes on to say, 'One day she accidentally met Dr Slach our GP and he felt she had TB. Luckily for her it wasn't TB but it was caused by working with TNT.' Later Molly's mum worked at the tank factory at Monk Bretton called Frazer's just off Burton Road.

By 1943 it was almost impossible for a woman under 45 to avoid 'doing their bit.' About 80 per cent of married women were engaged in some sort of war work.

Supporting women with children, Yorkshire's first day nursery was to be opened on New Street, Barnsley, to offer day care for babies and infants. At a cost of a shilling per day, women employed in war work could leave their children from 7 am to 7 pm. Comprising an asphalt playground, lawn and sandpit the children would have been supervised by a matron, nurse, four probation nurses, one teacher and kitchen staff. The dreaded cod liver oil was administered daily. The youngest child was Michael Ferrington, aged 10 months. Two more nurseries were opened at Burton Grange and Wilthorpe. As a social experiment the nurseries were not as successful as first thought, despite their importance during the war. Mothers became indispensable in armament, equipment and engineering factories throughout Britain, however, for some reason nurseries were not popular in the West Riding area.

THE PHONEY WAR ENDS   133

WAR-TIME DAY NURSERIES.

THE War-time Day Nurseries in GREENFOOT LANE, WILTHORPE, BARNSLEY, and in LANG AVENUE, BURTON GRANGE, BARNSLEY, are now open for the reception of Children between the ages of 6 months and 5 years.

THE NURSERIES are open from 7 a.m. to 7 p.m. on Monday to Friday, and from 7 a.m. to 1 p.m. on Saturdays.

Parents who desire their children admitting to the Nurseries should make application direct to the Nursery at any time.

FEES: 1/- per day.

A. E. GILFILLAN,
Town Clerk.

Wartime daytime nursery.

In response to women wanting to work, nurseries were one of the first social experiments of the war. Nurseries were opened in Barnsley but evidently were not popular.

134 BARNSLEY AT WAR 1939–45

Stairfoot child welfare centre with Mayoress Walton where she was a regular helper. (Barnsley Chronicle)

Fireman Jack Hazzard, who died when he fell from the Town Hall.

Another notable event in December was the start of Yorkshire Warship Campaign, which had already raised enough money for fourteen boats of several types including two destroyers.

For the family of Leading Fireman Jack Hazzard, 1941 ended in tragedy. A large crowd had gathered at the Town Hall to witness a hands-on demonstration by the Fire Service. Men, women and children stood watching 40 feet above them as Jack fell to his death. Firemen operating a turntable extending ladder were waiting for Jack to climb to the balcony of the Town Hall. After 'rescuing' him they lowered him to the ground by means of a rope fastened under his armpits. A witness who was operating the machinery had not lowered him more than a foot when he noticed that one of the pawls was fast. He recalled in his evidence to the coroner, 'I extended the ladder to release the pawl and having done this I lowered him about 20 feet when the rope broke and he fell to the walkway below.' The coroner recorded a verdict of death by misadventure and no one was found guilty of negligence; however, questions were asked about the type of rope and its fixings.

The town's third wartime Christmas was celebrated quietly with miners enjoying a three-day break, to the annoyance of some who only wanted them to have Christmas day off.

January to June 1942

In January 1942 a Whitley bomber piloted by Alexander 'Bruno' Hollingworth of the Royal Australian Airforce crashed at Pogmoor. Alex was the son of William Alexander and Maude Hollingworth of Bowen Hills, Brisbane. People could see as the burning bomber flew over the town with some of the crew bailing out. The Whitney carried on its flight until the pilot put the burning plane down at the clay pit quarry near Cresswell Street, Pogmoor. Alex died in the crash, as did Wireless Operator/Air Gunner Sergeant Alexander Gibson Buchanan of the RCAF when he left it too late to bail out. In detail this is what happened to Whitley bomber Z9289: On 6 January 1942 this 102 Squadron aircraft took off from Dalton airfield at 04.24 hours for an operational flight to attack Cherbourg docks and was one of four from this squadron to fly the operational order on this night but one did not take off because of engine trouble on the ground at Dalton. The crew of Whitley Z9289 were unable to locate the target area because of thick cloud so did not release their bombs, while over the French target the starboard engine began to give the crew trouble so they made for home. On their flight up England the engine over-revved uncontrollably so it was shut down. The aircraft began losing height flying on just one engine. Believing they could be over high ground the crew jettisoned the bomb load – this turned out to be over an area around twelve miles south-west of Sheffield. The aircraft continued to lose height, so the pilot opted to restart the failed engine; this resulted in it catching fire. The pilot then ordered his crew to abandon the aircraft over the Barnsley area, but he remained at the controls so that it would not crash amongst housing. With the engine on fire the aircraft crashed at 10.10 hours. The former quarry was being used as a tip for coal ash at the time and the aircraft crashed into the ash. The parachute of Sergeant Buchanan failed to deploy properly as he left it too late to make the jump; his parachute caught on the chimney of a cottage next to a refuse incinerator. Three others survived, landing nearby. Hollingworth was a hero that chilly day; long may he be remembered for averting a disaster that could have claimed far more lives.

Above: Alexander Hollingworth was born in Brisbane in January 1919; he enlisted for RAAF service there. The flight in which he died in Barnsley was his first as an operational captain.

Left: Rose Hill Cemetery, Doncaster, the final resting place for the brave Australian pilot.

Early in 1942 news arrived of a Japanese offensive in Burma. By now sons and daughters of Barnsley had gone out to various parts of the world, such as ex-pat Dorothy (Dolly) Carr née Haigh who lived at 108 Blenheim Road. Her husband had worked for Burma Oil since 1937. Dolly, who was known locally as an accomplished swimmer, now lived in a bungalow at Khodaung in Burma. She got out in the nick of time leaving all her possessions behind making it to India along the Burma Road. Dolly travelled by plane, steamer, train and on foot to finally reach Bombay.

Another ex-pat, Gilbert Vickers, formerly of Cockerham Avenue, also worked for Burma Oil and lived at Nyhunghia in Burma with his wife and young son. Both families were in a precarious situation as the Imperial Japanese army, with aid from the Royal Thai Armed Forces and Burmese insurgents, were about to drive the British and Chinese forces out of Burma. Terrifying and unpredictable times lay ahead for the families. But they got out alive and made it safely back to England.

THE PHONEY WAR ENDS

The first Royston man to win a medal in this war was reported to be Flight Sergeant Roland Edmonds, son of Arthur of 108 Station Road. He was awarded the DFM for his 'brilliant work and devotion to duty in bombing Brest'.

January 1942 was the start of Barnsley's Warship Week, which eventually raised £625,647 to sponsor a submarine: HMS *Regent*, famous for her valiant work in the Kotor Harbour. Her eventual fate was 10 miles north of the Italian city Barletta. Just off the rocky shore in the sea sits a replica of the Barnsley coat of arms attached to the submarine which was sunk while patrolling the Adriatic in 1943. Amongst its crew was a Ryhill seaman, Leading Stoker Jeffrey Hudson of Churchfields. Jeffrey and his crewmates died when the submarine hit a mine. One theory is that on 18 April *Regent* struck a mine north of Barletta after attacking an Italian convoy. It was reported that earlier that day an unidentified submarine had attempted to torpedo the small Italian tanker *Bivona*: the submarine may have been *Regent*. A second theory was that the submarine was north of Monopoli, further along the same coast, where she fired a torpedo at the merchant vessel *Baltic* but missed. The Italian corvette *Gabbiano* was escorting *Baltic* and immediately launched a depth charge attack, which it was thought could have destroyed *Regent*.

Dolly Carr endured the Burma ordeal just before the Japanese attacked.

HMS Regent, *the Barnsley-sponsored submarine that sank in 1943.*

138   BARNSLEY AT WAR 1939–45

Above: (Worsbrough Warship Week).

Left: January 1942 Warship Week.

Below: Ryhill Stoker Jeffrey Hudson on the Barnsley sponsored submarine HMS Regent.

THE PHONEY WAR ENDS   139

Darton Warship week – this model torpedo boat, which toured Darton, was built around a car. It must have looked strange sailing along the road.

A little-known Act was the registration of Boys and Girls Order 1941. Any boy or girl who failed to register in accordance with the Act would be liable to prison or a £100 fine. Registration points were administered throughout the borough. The registration started in a bitterly cold January, just before the next object of rationing: soap!

Between 8 and 15 February, fighting in the Far East and Singapore had been vicious. Barnsley folk still out there found themselves in precarious situations. Some stationed there had their families with them. Sergeant Peter Derbyshire of Kendray was one, with his wife, three daughters and one son. Another was Gunner Douglas Ratcliffe, RA, of 8 Lane Cottages, Church Street, Royston. He was fortunate to be able to send his wife Irene a cable informing her of his safety despite Singapore falling to the Japanese. Irene, who came from Manchester, was working on munitions.

In February a horrific incident at Barnsley Main Colliery claimed thirteen victims. There was a rush of volunteers for the dangerous work of rescue, and one man taking a 'sick note' to No. 2 pit, hearing of the disaster, hurried over to No. 4 pit and volunteered to do what he could, going down the mine to help. He described how 'men were falling over themselves to volunteer… I went down and helped carry some of the injured men out. Rescue workers were bringing the injured nearly to the pit bottom, and then we took over. The men were as cool as cucumbers and appeared more concerned about their workmates injuries than about themselves.' One of the stretcher bearers was Charlie Hardcastle, former featherweight champion of England and holder of the Lonsdale Belt who worked at the colliery at the time of the disaster. Councillor Richards (secretary of Barrow-Barnsley Main Collieries Ltd) told a reporter, 'the rescue workers and the stretcher bearers were magnificent, in fact so they were all.' Barnsley's Civil Defence services rendered valuable help and a fleet of ARP ambulances and first aid parties were diverted to help at the chaotic scenes. As darkness descended, anxious relatives flocked to the scene eagerly waiting news of their husbands and sons. It was late in the evening when the bodies were finally brought out from the pit.

The origin of the disaster appears to go back to 16 February when all the men were evacuated because of a fire. Officially the inquiry described the problem thus: 'I am of the opinion that the electric trailing cable was not sufficiently examined when it arrived at the face and before the current was turned on. I understand that the regulations provide that such a cable must be examined once by the cutter-man in each shift, but there has been no evidence that this was done in this case, and it seems to me that it would be well if the regulations were amended to provide for a proper examination by instrument at the commencement of each shift before the power is put on.'[14]

The Barnsley Main Colliery Disaster Fund was set up by the mayor for the families of the thirteen dead and the many others injured.

'Women at the Wheel' was the headline in early April when eight conductresses of the YTC commenced duties as drivers after six months of training. The women displayed good road sense and thoroughly acquired the 'art of smooth gear changing in their single decker buses'. Since the war began the company had lost the services of sixty-eight male drivers, some called up for military service, others into other industries. Offsetting some reduction of services there was a corresponding increase in special buses to munition works, collieries, etc.

On Sunday, 12 April, The Right Hon. Ernest Bevin, member of the War Cabinet and Minister of Labour and National Service, spoke in Royston at the Palace Cinema, introduced by 'Keep the Home Fires Burning' played by the Home Guard Band. He spoke of productivity targets and about the importance of miners going to work. Barnsley magistrates' courts were inundated with cases of men in breach of the Essential Work Order 1941 who had failed to turn up for work. One case stands out: that of the unusually-named Royal Butterwood of Monk Bretton. Royal was sent to prison after being reported to the Minister of Labour by the Pit Production Committee at Woolley Colliery where he was a bricklayer. He had been absent from work 52 per cent of the time he could have worked. His wife Lillian called the Labour Exchange and said the defendant would not work because he was 'too idle'. Strong words were said by Walter Gledhill, National Service Officer, who expressed the opinion that Royal was a shirker. 'He was physically fit but would not work, this is one of the worst cases I have had.' Royal had not learned his lesson, and a few months later he was in front of the tribunal again. This time, asked if he intended working, he said, 'I should go to work if I had an alarm clock to get up with.' In Barnsley during the '40s it was customary for a man with a long pole to

THE PHONEY WAR ENDS   141

MINISTRY OF INFORMATION
LOCAL INFORMATION COMMITTEE
Saturday, April 12th, 1942, Doors Open 10.30 a.m.
PALACE CINEMA, ROYSTON
ADDRESS BY
Mr. ERNEST BEVIN
Minister of Labour & National Service
Chairman - Mr. George Griffiths, M.P.

1018

THE YORKSHIRE TRACTION COMPANY LIMITED

We Are At Our Wits End

trying to provide all the necessary Travel Facilities for Workpeople.

Owing to Women Shoppers Travelling Before 9-0 a.m.

Hundreds of Workpeople are having to put up with unnecessary inconvenience and discomfort.

We Are Severely Rationed For Petrol And Fuel Oil

AND WE APPEAL TO THE LADIES TO HELP US.

UPPER SHEFFIELD ROAD.
BARNSLEY.   Tel. 2476.

N. H. DEAN,
General Manager.

RAT MENACE in BARNSLEY and WOMBWELL

Every man, woman, and child is asked to be a "Rat-Reporter"

Rats are a growing danger! They are at an alarming level right in this district.

A country-wide effort is being made to destroy these food-devouring, disease-spreading pests. The campaign is in full swing locally this month. Will you report any stray rats you see?

HOW TO REPORT

If you see rats anywhere in this neighbourhood, or know where there are any, please report them in one of these ways, whichever is easiest for you:

EITHER

FILL IN COUPON BELOW and take or post it (unsealed envelope, 1d. stamp) to the Public Health Department. (See address on coupon.)

OR

WRITE FULL DETAILS ON A CARD or piece of paper and take or post it to the Public Health Department. (See address on coupon.)

OR

TELEPHONE THE PUBLIC HEALTH DEPARTMENT (See telephone number on the coupon below.) Ask to speak to the Rat Officer.

Your report, along with other people's, will help the experts to make a map showing where the main nests of rats are in this area, so they can be tracked down and destroyed by the thousands.

Of course, if there are rats on your own property, it is still your responsibility to see they are destroyed. But join the Rat-Reporters, too!

Start today. Keep a sharp look-out for rats, and report all you see. Help to win the war on rats!

COUPON — FOR CONVENIENCE. If you see a rat, fill in this coupon and take or post it (or write a card) to:

Health Dept., Town Hall, Barnsley (Tele: ...)
Sanitary Inspector's Dept., Town Hall, Wombwell (Tele: ...)

I have seen rats, or traces of rats, on _____ (give date)

at _____

_____ (give exact location)

Signature _____

Address _____

Rats were considered a serious menace during the war. In 1940 there where an estimated 50 million rats in Britain. During harvest they would live under the stacks and cobs of drying crops then move into barns and stores during winter where they would devour the crop. The Land Girls christened the rats 'Hitler's little helpers' and were paid a bonus for every rat they caught, usually one or two pence a tail.

knock on windows to alert men that their shift was about to start – he must have forgotten Royal that morning. More about Royal later.

This was at a time when the Yorkshire Coalfield needed 15,000 more men to meet demand. Bevin called it 'the second front'. In 1943 part of Silkstone Golf course was taken over for opencast mining which produced 100,000 tons of coal. It was not until 1956 that the course was finally restored.

The year 1942 was volatile for the mining industry, with various demands, stoppages, appeals and government action, the position fluctuating day by day. It could be argued that the miners deserved more pay, considering the long hours and the dangers. Striking in a time of national crisis was, however, not popular. One person wrote in the *Chronicle*, 'we feel that the miners who strike at this critical time are a disgrace to Yorkshire, and their unpatriotic conduct will be remembered long after the war is over.' Later in the year men under the age of 25 when registering for service would be given the opportunity to either work underground in the mines or join the armed forces.

Barnsley considered Russia to be a worthy ally and the town poured thousands of pounds into the Russia Fund. In Russia the Germans were on the brink of defeat and the Socialist council endeavoured to supply whatever they could to the country. Three thousand guineas were presented to Ivan Maisky, ambassador

MINISTRY OF INFORMATION

ANGLO-SOVIET CAMPAIGN

IN ASSOCIATION WITH THE PUBLICITY AND CULTURAL RELATIONS COMMITTEE OF THE

MAYOR OF BARNSLEY'S AID-TO-RUSSIA FUND

THE

LOCAL INFORMATION COMMITTEE

HAVE ARRANGED FOR

Mrs. WILLIAMS-ELLIS

(who has travelled extensively in Russia before and since the Revolution)

TO ADDRESS A MEETING IN THE

MINERS' HALL, BARNSLEY

ON

THURSDAY, OCTOBER 22nd

at 7 p.m.

ADMISSION FREE, by Ticket, to be obtained from members of the Local Information Committee, and Mrs. Park, 56, Park Grove, Barnsley.

(Russian fund)

Ivan Maisky, Russian ambassador to London, received a cheque from the Mayor for the Russian fund.

to the Russian Embassy in London, by the mayor, his wife and others from the council in November 1942. Through the Anglo-Soviet Relations Committee, the town even considered adopting a Russian town.

In April the Germans planned the 'Baedeker raids', on touristy or historic British sites, in revenge for the Lübeck bombing. Early in the morning on Wednesday, 29 April 1942, York suffered its worst air raid of the war. It wasn't entirely unexpected. In the previous few days, the Luftwaffe had attacked two other cathedral cities, Norwich and Bath. Unopposed for much of the raid, the Germans dive-bombed and strafed the streets with machine gun fire. They also bombarded some strategic targets: the railway and station, the carriage works and the airfield. York Minster was not touched. The raid left ninety-two people dead and hundreds injured. One of the dead was a Barnsley airman, Bernard Hawcroft, while another Barnsley airman, Flight Mechanic Herbert Leslie, 34, of 7 Nursery Street, had a fortunate escape after been buried for three hours under the wreckage of a four-storey building which received a direct hit.

In April, West Riding Home Guard battalions were asked to man anti-aircraft batteries. Each battery consisted of several reliefs, and a considerable number of men were required. They worked in close co-operation with the units and formations of Anti-Aircraft Command and the local Home Guard battalions. Local gun pits included one on Kexborough School playing fields for the regular army. At weekends the regular army trained the Home Guard and the WVS did the cooking.

The Evening Press *lino room the morning after the Baedeker raid on York.* (Yorkshire Evening Press – Ian Cottom)

Members of the ATS operating the huge searchlights.

Another Ack-Ack pit was at Bolton-upon-Dearne, just south-east of Lowfield Farm, as part of a ring of defences called the 'ring of steel' to protect Sheffield against bombing. It was a heavy gun site designated Station H17. The now derelict site includes four gun emplacements, a command post, a Nissen hut at the entrance and part of the old service track.[15]

Janet Lancaster mentioned the Nissen huts in her reminiscences of Bolton: 'I lived opposite the Angel Hotel from 1940 to 1955. There were several farms in Bolton and most of the farmers had children my age, so I spent many happy hours in the farm yards and country lanes. My best friend Anne Beaumont was a farmer's daughter. I remember her dad offering us a shilling each if we would hoe the weeds down in one of his fields. This we did, and he transported us home on his tractor, sitting on the mudguards. Health and safety was unheard of in those days. I also have a memory of walking down Station Road with Mike and John Palfreman when they were taking a herd of cows from the farm to the fields. I also remember the Nissen huts down Station Road, and squatters living in them after the war. Those people must have been desperate to live in those conditions. I wonder if they were there in the icy cold winter of 1947.'

In North Africa anxious relatives of soldiers serving in Libya were at home waiting for news after the reversal at Tobruk. The Fishers who were fruiterers of Wombwell and the Watlings of Barnsley being two families who were caught up in the Battle of Gazala. Scores of Barnsley men were reported missing. Ironically the town at the time was celebrating the inception of the United Nations, an organisation made to bring peace and security to the world. The flags were carried in a parade from the Queen's Grounds to Locke Park on Sunday, 28 June 1942. It was part of a two-mile-long parade for the annual memorial service in remembrance of Barnsley's heroes of the Somme twenty-six years before.

Another gas mask drill took place in Hoyland when Civil Defence released tear gas in the main street of Hoyland at 10.30 pm. Despite notices being posted for ten days advising of the release some people took offence. An incensed, hostile crowd numbering 800 to 1,000 collected in front of the police station and Ernest Mott, John W. Steeples and Lawrence Davies incited the them to charge at the office and get at the officers. Stones were thrown, the station door was kicked in and Steeples rushed at PC Sanders and called upon the crowd to follow him. He struck several blows at Sanders, who closed with him and tried to get him into the police station. Davies then ran up and struck War Reserve Constable Fletcher who was assisting Sanders. After this the crowd became unruly, and things began to look ominous, so much so that at one point Sergeant Moran feared it would be necessary to make a baton charge. As all efforts to get the crowd to disperse failed, Sergeant Moran placed an ignited gas canister in front of the station. Mott then ran up and kicked the canister underneath a stationary car, which might have been set on fire had not Moran kicked the canister from under the car. Mott picked up the canister and hurled it back at the sergeant hitting him on the outlet valve of his respirator. The police described it as the worst exhibition of hooliganism they had ever seen.

August to December 1942

August started with the dismantling of the old Monk Bretton Station, with the booking office and waiting room being transformed into a place of worship.

Then Edric Townend was killed by a bomb during a practice at Cawthorne Basin. Edric Clifford Townend, 49, of Limesway, Gawber, originally from Darton, a sergeant in the Staincross Home Guard who served in the Great War as a sergeant with the Y&L, left a wife, Edith, and two children. Ernest Sykes, a lance corporal of Vaughan Road, Gawber, said he was waiting for his turn to throw the practice grenade. John Mason, a comrade of Edric, picked up the bomb to throw it down the embankment. He heard Edric give the orders and then he saw the explosion. The command and the explosion followed almost immediately after the grenade left Mason's hand. Both Mason and Townend fell back into the trench. A bomb of this type would normally take about four seconds to explode once the fuse had been set. An eye witness said, 'the story of these men will be told by those who saw it long after this war has faded into the distant past, and they will be proud, as I am, to be able to say, "We are their pals." If ever the calls come for us to suffer, may we be able to take it with the same courage and gallantry as MEN LIKE THESE.' Edric's gravestone at All Saints Churchyard, Darton, reads, 'In the midst of life we are in death.'

The Dieppe Raid took place on 19 August 1942. Stalin had encouraged the formation of a second front in the west, so socialists in Barnsley supported the idea. The assault began at 5 am, and by 10.50 am the Allied commanders were forced to call a retreat. Involved were 5,000 Canadians of the Calgary Regiment of the 1st Canadian Tank Brigade, 1,000 British of the Royal Navy and some smaller Royal Air Force landing contingents, and 50 US Army Rangers.

Corporal George Renshaw (22), a Royal Marine Commando of Doncaster Road, and John

John Miller, a Royal Marine Commando who took part in the Dieppe raids.

Miller of Sheffield Road took part, and survived. Rigid censorship prevented the press from revealing details of the failed raid. Dieppe was only a success in that lessons were learned from it.

Registration day for males between 18 and 60 and females between 20 and 45 for fire prevention duties was 26 September 1942. Persons exempt would be those already in Civil Defence or in the Armed Forces.

Church bells rang throughout the borough to celebrate the Allied victory at El Alamein which prevented the Axis army advancing further into Egypt. It coincided with the mayor's parade and the inauguration of the new mayor, Sam Trueman.

Heroic accounts of Barnsley men were still being recorded as the year ended, such as the Barnsley glassworker who had been twice torpedoed crossing the Atlantic. Gunner Percy Ruston of Redfearn Street considered himself lucky to be picked up by ships nearby from the cold sea.

Another thrilling experience was recalled by Stairfoot Stoker Horace Owen (KX148489), whose ship HMS *Hecla* was sunk off Casablanca on Armistice Day 1942. After a terrific explosion, all the lights went out and there was a dash for

(Courtesy of Bill Forster and holywellhousepublishing.co.uk/A_Hard_Fought_Ship.html)

HMS Hecla *left Freetown in west Africa as part of Convoy CF.7A on 4 November 1942 and was photographed by Tom Davis, the ship's writer on HMS* Active. *(Courtesy of Steve Davis, stepson of Tom Davis)*

the relative safety of the upper deck. A torpedo had struck the boiler room on the starboard side. After a few minutes Carley floats were dropped into the sea. The order was made to abandon ship and survivors made their way to a nearby destroyer, which was itself hit by a torpedo. While in the water depth chargers went off causing severe pain in the stomach of Horace and the other men. Horace swam to another ship and was one of the first men to be picked up. Thirty minutes later they were again in action because the submarine had surfaced some 200 yards away and they fired on it. About 300 survivors were picked up by one destroyer and 60 by another. Sources record 799 ratings and 39 officers as being on HMS *Hecla*, of which 556 were rescued, including another Barnsley sailor Cyril Hardware, Electrical Artificer 4th Class. HMS *Marne* rescued 64 before a torpedo blew off her stern but most, 493, were saved by HMS *Venomous* despite her having to break off to attack the U-boat.[16] Cyril's experience can be read about in the *Barnsley Chronicle*, 26 December 1942, page 6.

By the end of 1942 Germany had suffered setbacks at Stalingrad and El Alamein and the American naval victory at Battle of Midway marked a turning point in the Pacific War.

Cyril B. Hardware, who survived the sinking of HMS Hecla.

CHAPTER 4

Seeing it Through

After the successes of 1942 there was cause for optimism on the war front. In Barnsley, miners were either working hard or striking, causing discord in the town. Yorkshire was still missing its output targets to the dissatisfaction of the War Cabinet. Eight hundred bus drivers got in on the act and caused a lightning strike impacting coal output forcing Army and RAF vehicles to supply the munition factories and mines with workers.

Juvenile crime was still on the increase with some expressing their 'disgust' at the hooligans who blighted the borough, a stark contrast to the youths who had joined the Armed Forces or those waiting in the wings in their chosen pre-service cadet force. Barnsley's first two youth clubs were set up in 1942 at Ardsley and Grove Street, followed by a third club which opened on Racecommon Road.

The first registration of under 18s was to happen on 9 January 1943. It applied to 50 per cent of boys and about 80 per cent of girls who were not affiliated with any youth movement. Interestingly, a sizeable proportion of the boys were already with the Home Guard.

Aircraftwoman 2nd Class Rieta Woodhall, one of the few female fatalities of the war who died after a shot to the chest via her wrist.

Female casualties from Barnsley were few in the war but an exception was Aircraftwoman 2nd Class Rieta Woodhall whose family lived at Shaw Lane, Barnsley. Her father worked at Fletcher's butchers before moving to Grimsby. Rieta was going off duty and had to pass through a guard room. An RAF corporal was examining a service revolver and just as Rieta was passing the gun went off. They were talking about the gun when the corporal placed a bullet in the chamber, and as Rieta reached for her bag she nudged the corporal who in turn let off the gun. Striking her left wrist, the bullet then entered her chest and fractured an artery. She was taken to hospital but died as she was being prepared for surgery. She was buried with full military honours at Hillingdon and Uxbridge Cemetery.

Nursing staff aboard troopships were legitimate targets for enemy planes. One troopship was the *Strathallan* that sailed from the Clyde with the staff of the general hospital. The *Strathallan* was torpedoed on a moonlit night in December 1942 taking some time to sink. During this time two Queen Alexandra sisters, Julia Kerr and Olive Stewardson from Grimethorpe, stayed in the sick bay to nurse five badly injured soldiers. Olive, who was making her first trip overseas, entered the nursing service in 1928, and trained at Huddersfield Royal Infirmary until 1932. She then joined the Territorial Nursing Service as a Queen Alexandra nurse and was in that service until the outbreak of war. The *Daily Express* reported the account of one James Wellard:

Olive Stewardson, a Queen Alexandra nurse who exceeded her duty onboard the troopship Strathallan.

I want you to meet five brave women, three English, two American. I want you to meet them as I saw them tonight – aboard a crippled transport torpedoed in the bright moonlight. As I write this we are sinking. Fire has broken out below

SS Strathallan *torpedoed by* U-562, *21 December 1942; 250 nurses and 4,000 troops are rescued.*

decks. The crump of a torpedo smacking the side of a big ship when you are fast asleep in your berth is a sound you don't want to hear more than once in your life. We, the nurses and soldiers, American and British, heard it in the night. When 29-year-old Olive Stewardson from Yorkshire and 26-year-old Julie Kerr, who is Irish, heard it they knew they had a duty to perform. They are Queen Alexandra nurses. That duty was in the troops' hospital deep down in the bowels of the ship. The rest of us stumbled up the dark stairs to our boat stations. We stood, some of us frightened, some of us singing, all of us calm and disciplined as befits soldiers. Sisters Stewardson and Kerr went down below decks while we went up. In the ship's hospital were five stretcher cases. The two sisters got them ready and saw them carried to safety. By this time the crowded lifeboats were away from the ship. There was no chance now for the nurses to leave except on rafts. Floating on a raft in a sea covered with fuel oil is the last resort, but the nurses had no thought of leaving. There was more work to do. Casualties were coming into that little hospital below decks. Sailors and soldiers covered in fuel oil and exhausted were being brought in every minute. Sisters Stewardson and Kerr carried on. They cut off the men's clothing, massaged them, hot water bottles at their feet. Late the next day the sisters came on deck, their work done. They found the sun shining bright and warm. The ship was listing 20 degrees. All the other nurses had left except 39-year-old Sister Judith Baskett and two American WAACs. Sister Baskett told me – 'I came up on deck with another sister and when we got to the lifeboat there was room for one only. I told the other sister to get in. The sisters wished me good-luck, and then they were gone.' For 32-year-old Loise Anderson of Denver and 33-year-old A. Dregmal of Wisconsin, there was no room either. Sitting on the deck of the doomed ship they were cheerful, trim and becomingly powdered and rouged. Well. Here is the story Sisters Stewardson and Kerr told me – 'When the torpedo hit we got dressed, put on our tin hats, collected our greatcoats and went to the troops' hospital on the lower deck. We found the medical officer and orderlies already there, strapping patients to the stretchers. Two of the men had broken legs. As soon as we had taken care of the stretcher cases we went upstairs. Then the casualties from the lifeboats and rafts were brought in. We were asked to go down to the hospital and take care of them. They were the soldiers and sailors who had jumped to the rafts; they were covered in fuel oil. Most of them were exhausted from exposure. We took off their clothes and rubbed them and did what we could. It was late next day – five hours later, when we came up on the top deck. They wrapped us in warm blankets. And here we are. And here we are, five women and hundreds of men a little anxious but confident the Royal Navy will not forget us. The ship is listing heavily. Fire has broken out. It is dangerous now to return below decks. But there is no sign of panic aboard. There never has been since we were torpedoed. Lifeboats of American and British nurses can be seen still bobbing on the horizon. I heard later from Sister Lorna Parker of Wiltshire this amazing story: – 'When our boat touched the water, it flooded almost immediately because someone had forgotten to put in the plug. We found ourselves in the water, so some of the other girls and I began to swim. A girl behind me shouted 'Where are you going?' I said, 'I'm going to such-and-such a place, just take the third wave to the right.' The 12 of us swam off together, striking out for the rafts. We clung on to these for three hours. I had many bad moments. No one can imagine how lonely it is swimming around in the ocean in the middle of the night. Once I felt something clinging to my legs. I put down my hand to feel, and fond an octopus wrapped around them. Several destroyers passed us in the night but could not see us. Finally, a destroyer came towards us. We all shouted together. It must have been a horrible noise, but the crew heard us. Soon we were safe on board. Sailors took off our clothes, which were covered in grease and oil, and washed them for us. We found them hanging on a line when we reached port.'

A sailor in the destroyer which picked up the twelve nurses said: 'I've seen and heard some strange things at sea, but the cries of those girls and the sight of them hanging to the raft as we bore down on them at 23 knots made my heart come into my mouth. I can't forget it.

'All of us saw sights we shall never forget. There was the moment when lifeboats, with nurses aboard, swung down from the davits and bobbed about in the moonlight water. There was the spectacle of Tommies and Doughboys standing on the listing ship singing; 'You are my sunshine' to the accompaniment of a mouth organ. There was that dry sandpaper feeling in the mouth and throat as you stood around for hours, waiting and wondering. There was the relief of sunrise, which had never seemed so beautiful before. There was the tense moment when you went over the side of the ship, dangling on a rope and praying for strength to hang on until you were dropped on the decks of a destroyer 40 feet below.

'There was the final tragic spectacle of your good ship, burning like a funeral pyre until she was just a smudge on the horizon.'

Olive was mentioned in dispatches in the *London Gazette* on 16 September 1943.

The Wings for Victory campaign started in earnest at the beginning of the year. One Lancaster Bomber and two Spitfires could be bought for £50,000. On the back of Warship Week in 1942 it was hoped that the Wings week would be just as successful. Smaller councils fixed their targets lower while Barnsley fixed theirs at £750,000. Wings for Victory coincided with various other celebrations in the town including the third anniversary of the Home Guard and the visit of Lady Louis Mountbatten and Sir John Maitland Salmon.

Back in the Atlantic a nightmare story follows eighteen men who took refuge in a lifeboat when their ship was torpedoed then sailed almost blindly into the North Atlantic's alternate storm and calm. All but three died. One of those adrift who survived the 21-day open-boat ordeal was Able Seaman Gunner Ernest Hill who lived at Old Mill Lane, Barnsley. A tough Yorkshire working man, Hill's hardy constitution, amazing courage and powers of endurance pulled him through. Before joining the Navy in March 1941, he was employed just down the road at Star Paper Mills. A well-travelled sailor, his wife received a telegram to say that

DODWORTH
Wings for Victory Week
MARCH 27th to APRIL 3rd, 1943

Target - £20,000
THE COST OF A WELLINGTON BOMBER

Opening Ceremony
on **Saturday, March 27th**
at 3 p.m. outside the Council Offices, by
Major W. J. TAYLOR
Deputy Lieutenant of the West Riding of Yorkshire, followed by
A GRAND PARADE including detachments of the W.A.A.F., the A.T.C., the A.C.C. and the W.J.A.C., as well as of all Local Services, and headed by the BAND of the BARNSLEY WING of the AIR TRAINING CORPS. Major W. J. TAYLOR will take the Salute.

INDICATOR CEREMONY each day at 6.30 p.m.

ATTRACTIVE PROGRAMME OF EVENTS THROUGHOUT THE WEEK. FOR DETAILS SEE OFFICIAL PROGRAMME, Price 3d.

SHOW YOUR GRATITUDE TO THE ROYAL AIR FORCE BY INVESTING YOUR MONEY DURING THIS WEEK.

Dodworth Wings for Victory week. The village exceeded its target, as it did for every special week.

he was missing, but an unexpected Christmas present brought glad tidings to the family saying that he had been picked up and was safe in New York. *The Bangor Daily News*, Maine, described it as 'one of the greatest stories of harrowing experiences as applied to a single group that emerged out of the War':

One by one his friends died and were buried in the sea. Never did they feel a moments peace nor even a moments hope. Never was there a time when they were not drenched to the skin for the North Atlantic is a relentless, unforgiving giant, even in calm and the boat was tossed as by some cosmic irony on its broad bosom. 21 days after being torpedoed and 650 miles away, four survivors – one of whom died a few hours afterwards – were lifted up the sides of a Norwegian freighter in the Atlantic.

Does God answer prayer? The one prayer offered by these desperate men was on the twelfth day when they gulped down their lost drop of fresh water. They prayed together. Not the same words. Each man mumbled his own. They had no leader, not even coherent enough to lead. God answered their prayer on the thirteenth day when the heavens opened for 10 hours. They caught a silver stream by letting it run down their tattered sail into the empty casks. This was their first and only prayer.

Days before, Ernest had left with the crew of a supply ship. Days later, the torpedoes struck and their ship slid into the dark sea carrying several of its crew to a watery grave. But two lifeboats had been launched. The submarine came to the surface and an officer on deck directed the boats to come alongside. 'Which one of you is captain?' he asked in perfect English. The captain identified himself and was forced onto the sub which then submerged offering no help to the crews in the boats. They were left to their own fate and Ernest's tiny craft, complete with sail drifted off into the darkness.

The boats kept together for a few hours and then drifted apart. Hill and his companions decided to head for Northern Ireland. In the boat they had some food, milk tablets and pemmican which is a meat in a highly concentrated form. Water was kept in three small casks. They rationed themselves from the first, three pieces of chocolate and a spoonful of meat at each meal. At first, they ate three times a day then reduced that to two and once daily a drink of that priceless water. They drank from a tiny tube which was eight inches long but which they never more than half filled.

On the second day they ran into a North West gale, and the 16-foot boat was tossed about getting thrown hopelessly off course. Death was very near as their little craft rose to the top of the waves to be slammed down into the troughs, which gave the sensation of falling from the side of a building. That was literally the lull before the storm as the next day was sunny but very cold and chilly. On this day the first man died, the oldest of the group at 50.

Two others died of exposure on the day following. There were no dramatic agonies or emotive speeches, just each man died quietly.

Time drifted by, the cold grey days eight hours or so long, then the all-engulfing darkness of the nights, three days there were three more deaths.

The boat, riding a slight swell, but no swell is really slight in the Atlantic, was steered towards the north east and their water was exhausted on the eleventh day. On the twelfth day for the first time they prayed as a group, the rain came just too late after another man died.

Six more days! The weather remained calm and the survivors kept to a north east course, getting their bearings from the sun, moon and stars. On the 17th day three others died, and the water in the casks was running dangerously low again. On the 19th day two wireless operators and an able seaman died.

The 20th day! Four seemingly doomed men drifted. Their water had gone.

Finally, on the 21st day salvation arrived. At 9.30 am the Norwegian ship that was to become their saviour loomed on the far horizon. With desperate eagerness the four sent up a smoke flare and the yellow vapour that was smeared across the sky was seen. The Norwegian had been about a mile and half away, but she drew alongside. Rope ladders were dropped over her sides and the four survivors were carried onboard, tragically one of those men died a few hours later.

Ernest lost fifty-eight pounds during the voyage.

Back at home, the No. 15 Platoon, D Company, 71st West Riding Battalion Home Guard had the distinction of beating 2,332 teams to win the English Home Guard Shooting Championship, the Mackworth Praed silver challenge cup. Hero of the shootout was Corporal Harold Holt, 33, a miner who a few days earlier had had his left hand crushed by a falling stone. Despite breaking bones and with his hand heavily bandaged he shot 10 bulls from 10 rounds. All were members of the Mapplewell Rifle Club.

Barnsley had about 400 soldiers, sailors and airmen incarcerated in PoW camps across the globe. Some fared better than others. Whatever conditions they found themselves in, there is no doubt the Barnsley Prisoners of War Association provided them whatever comfort they could. Its headquarters was at 15 Eldon Street before moving to Regent Street. For some it was the trivial things that

Staincross Home Guard – the man on the front is possibly Harold Holt whose hand was crushed by a fall of stone. Despite that he scored full marks to win the English Home Guard Shooting Championship.

reminded them of home, like a local newspaper or a cigarette. Mayor Trueman opened a toy and gift shop in the Arcade to raise funds for the men, £575 was raised in total.

Still in Barnsley an appalling discovery was made on Tuesday, 4 May, when Land Army worker Violet Wakefield was found inside the dodgems enclosure on Barnsley fairground between the Wellington Hotel and Wire Trellis Hotel with severe head injuries. Barely alive, she was huddled on the ground just inside the darkened entrance. Coming out of her caravan, Annie Tuby, proprietor of the dodgems, was checking all was well when she looked inside discovering Violet's blood-stained body. Immediately Annie called for assistance and Violet was taken to Becketts in a critical condition. She died later that day without regaining consciousness, with her parents by her side. At first the police thought she had been there overnight, however, a bus ticket for that morning was found on her person. Violet travelled from Cudworth on her way to Cawthorne Basin to work on a nearby farm. She had agreed to meet her boyfriend, Trevor Elvin, a glassworks engineer who lived at Grove Street. It was during that meeting Elvin hit her with a hammer several times, leaving her for dead. Elvin was later picked up in Blackpool and arrested for murdering the pretty Land Girl. Trevor Elvin was found guilty of the crime and hanged in Leeds for the horrific crime that caused a huge stir and front-page headlines in the borough.

One defining raid of the war, immortalised in book, film and music, is that of Operation Chastise, or the Dambusters of 617 Squadron. Again a Barnsley man was in the thick of the action, his name was Flight Engineer Sergeant David Horsfall. For many years a small group of Dutch citizens, headed by Jan van Dalen, have looked after the graves of the crew of Squadron Leader Melvin Young in the general cemetery of the small coastal town of Bergen. The crew were aboard Lancaster ED887, AJ-A, on the dam's raid on 16-17 May 1943, and all seven members lost their lives when they were shot down on their return journey. AJ-A had been the fourth aircraft to drop its Upkeep mine at the Mohne Dam and had caused a small breach. A few minutes later AJ-J dropped another mine, causing the final breach and the dam's collapse. Young had flown on to the Eder Dam to take over command if anything should happen to Guy Gibson on the attack there,

Dambuster David Taylor Horsfall was born in Bramley, Yorkshire, on 16 April 1920. The family moved to Barnsley and both he and his brother Albert went to Barnsley Grammar School.

but in the event he had nothing to do. He then set course to return home and reached the Dutch coast just before three in the morning. Out over the sea, he hit disaster when the gun battery at Wijk-aan-Zee fired at the rapidly disappearing Lancaster. At that stage, the aircraft was well past the last gun battery and only

Lancaster ED887, AJ-A. At 02.58 AJ-A crashed south of Castricum aan Zee. All seven crew were killed and washed ashore between Wijk-aan-Zee and Egmond-aan-Zee, the last at Castricum-aan-Zee on 30 May 1943. They are buried at Bergen General Cemetery.

a few hundred yards from safety. The battery later reported shooting down an aircraft at 0258, which was almost certainly AJ-A. Over the next few weeks, the sea yielded up the victims. Part of the wreckage was washed ashore and the first bodies – those of Melvin Young and David Horsfall – floated up on 29 May. They were buried two days later and were joined by the bodies of the other five which were washed up over the next thirteen days.

David Horsfall had a brother, Albert, who had been killed in 1940 serving as a navigator in 50 Squadron. The Horsfall family shared with the Taerums and the Minchins the unwanted distinction of having two sons killed on active air force service during the war.

Back home, the government sent out a call for 50,000 miners for the national coal fields, which was a prelude to the Bevin Boys coming to Barnsley: 12,000 of the 50,000 were required for the Yorkshire area.

Private Mavis Eames, an 18-year-old in the ATS, had the honour of being one of three Yorkshire girls in their class who were expert spotters of aircraft. Mavis could identify more than forty different of planes at any angle in the sky. She lived at Cross Lane, Royston, and joined the ATS in February 1942 when she volunteered. She was on the gun sight when Private Nora Caveney was the first ATS girl to be killed. Mavis herself had a narrow escape when she was hit on her tin helmet during a raid in the south. She was involved in heavy raids in London and several towns on the south coast. When the V-1s were being sent across the Channel many of the batteries moved to what was known as 'doodlebug alley'.

Private Mavis Eames, an 18-year-old in the ATS, was one of three Yorkshire girls who were expert spotters of aircraft.

HMS Polyanthus *that was sunk by* U-952 *on 21 September 1943 with two Barnsley souls on board.*

Particularly poignant are the deaths of two sailors aboard HMS *Polyanthus* on 21 September 1943. Just after midnight on a dark autumn night in the North Atlantic two Barnsley men perished together. Signalman Kenneth Wilton lived on Huddersfield Road and his shipmate Able Seaman Leslie Gordon Hardware lived at Wilthorpe Green. On the night of 19/20 September 1943, two westbound Convoys, ONS18 and ON 202, were facing frequent U-boat engagements. *Polyanthus* was called to their aid several times, including when *Escapade* and *Lagan* were nearly destroyed. After successfully driving away *U-238*, *Polyanthus* was ordered to rescue the crew from the escort HMCS *St. Croix*, recently sunk by *U-305*. Before any rescue could be effected, *Polyanthus* was sunk by *U-952* using a GNAT. At least seven officers and seventy-seven crew were lost with *Polyanthus*. The only known survivor drowned a few days later when the boat that rescued him, HMS *Itchen*, was sunk by another U-boat. Leslie's luck had run out that night: in December 1939 when he was serving aboard HMS *Belfast* it was struck by a torpedo and mine in the Firth of Forth; two years later he was on HMS *Delight* when that was sunk after an air attack.

Operation Source was a series of attacks to disrupt the capability of the heavy German warships *Tirpitz*, *Scharnhorst* and *Lützow* based in northern Norway, using X-class midget submarines. Stoker William Oxley was in submarine *X6*, named *Piker II*, commanded by Lieutenant Donald Cameron, which, along with *X5* and *X7*, were responsible for destroying the *Tirpitz*. The X Craft were towed by large submarines to their destinations where they could slip under anti-torpedo nets to each drop two 2-ton mines on the sea bed under the target. Ten vessels were assigned to the operation, scheduled for 20-25 September 1943. Only eight of the vessels reached Norway for the attack, which began early on 22 September. Three – *X5*, *X6*, and *X7* – successfully breached *Tirpitz*'s defences, two of which – *X6* and *X7* – managed to lay their mines. *X5* was detected some 600 feet from the nets and sunk by a combination of gunfire and depth charges. Although not sunk, *Tirpitz* was severely damaged and put out of action until April 1944.

Stoker William Oxley attacked the Tirpitz *in a midget submarine.*

Aerial view of Altenfjord and Kåfjord, showing Tirpitz *(see arrow) and the approximate route taken by X-5, X-6 and X-7.*

162 BARNSLEY AT WAR 1939–45

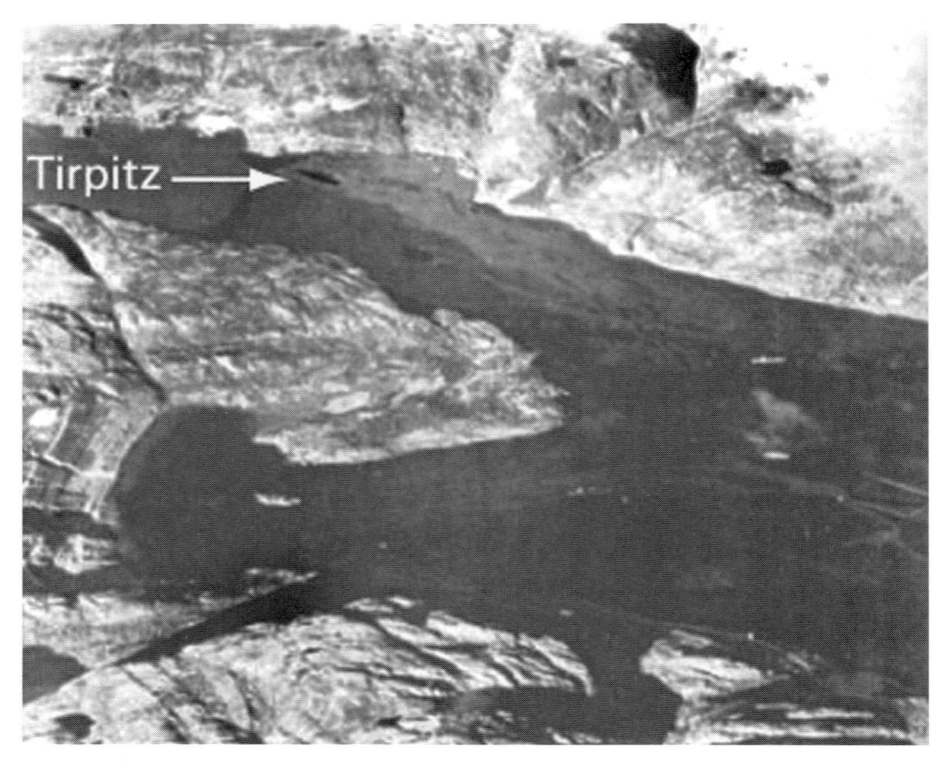

Taken shortly after the attack, showing Tirpitz *and other German vessels in Kåfjord and Altenfjord. Note the oil slicks in the water.*

Nurse lighting the fag of an injured 'Tommy' who was repatriated from Germany and returned on the Atlantis.

In Liverpool good news arrived on the ship *Atlantis* as it arrived at the Prince's Landing Stage in October 1943. She was carrying 764 badly injured Allied servicemen repatriated after being released from German prison camps. They included Flight Sergeant William Wetherill who had lost the use of his right hand, Alfred Hodder from Cawthorne whose ship sank in 1941, Alfred Crossland of Worsbrough Bridge who got back in time to see his seriously ill mum before she died, Sergeant Stanley Basil Birt of the Coldstream Guards who had lost his right foot, Sergeant John Robinson of Cudworth, Ronald Cooper of Shafton, Harold Haigh of Princess Street, Staincross, who had lost his left arm, Private Lewis John Afford, and a member of the Ambulance Unit, John Graham Wood. The hospital ships *Atlantis, Empress of Russia* and the *Drottingholm*, with 4,340 war prisoners, sailed from Gothenburg in the last week in October. The injured men had endured agonising tension, for they had experienced the bitterness of hope deferred when negotiations broke down two years before. Eager men were straining their eyes towards the west coast city hoping to catch a glimpse of Blighty. A chorus of all ranks sang out 'Roll out the Barrel', 'It's a long way to Tipperary' and other patriotic songs.

Luke Exley, a Barnsley private of the Sherwood Foresters who was injured at Dunkirk and one of the first soldiers to be repatriated in Barnsley.

Luke Exley, a Barnsley private of the Sherwood Foresters, also had this experience. Luke was the son of William and Elizabeth of Rebecca Street, where his wife Edna Jean lived with their two children. He was reported missing at Dunkirk and it later transpired that he was a prisoner and wounded, a shot having penetrated his ankle in Belgium which resulted paralysis on his left side. He was admitted to Camp Stalag IXAIH. In November 1941 he was passed by a German doctor as unfit for further military activity and put down for repatriation before those negotiations broke down. Three and half years later Edna Jean had received the joyous news that Luke was to return. Luke's life was already colourful before his time with the BEF when as a regular he married his wife who was a Channel Islander. After their marriage at Bullford, near Salisbury, both went to live in Guernsey. On the outbreak of the war they came to England with their children and as a reservist Luke rejoined his old regiment and went to France with the Foresters. He was a former pupil of Racecommon Road School. 'It does not seem to have changed much but I'm very glad to be home', said Luke. He described his experience: 'It was about 22 months before I received any proper treatment.

The Empress Atlantis *sailing towards the docks and home for the injured soldiers.*

I was five months in Belgium, then moved to a small hospital in Germany. Here conditions were rotten, meals consisting of a small piece of black bread and potato water. I was there 10 months then to a camp hospital, and from there was sent to Obermassfelt, a general hospital for PoWs where I received electrical treatment.' Luke said he was then moved to Klosterhiana, a recuperating centre, before he was sent home. The conditions at his new home were much better with 'proper equipment and decent food.' Describing the journey home, Private Exley said, 'We left Klosterhiana at 11.30 am on Monday and went to port on the coast of the Baltic. We boarded a ship and were taken to Sweden.' From there he went to Gothenburg where they were joined by a German destroyer which guided them through the minefields and so across the Atlantic to Liverpool.

Looking fit and happy and wearing the medal ribbons given them on the liner *Gripsholm*, many of the less severely wounded repatriated men went on leave.

Private Hiram Marrison, 27, of Barnsley Road, Cudworth, another of the returned prisoners said about his experience, 'The Germans were always asking when the invasion was going to come off. They never

Private Hiram Marrison, another of the returned prisoners who the town welcomed back.

talked when more than two were together, but on their own they would say, we are finished... When we were first taken prisoner the Hitler salute was being given all day long. Towards the end it was hardly ever seen. We could buy an Iron Cross Second Class for 20 cigarettes.' Hiram was captured in Crete and taken to a prison camp near Munich. He went on: 'We heard plenty of our boy's air raids and when they came over there was much excitement in our camp. The bombs never came near the camps so the German civilians living nearby used to use the trenches at the camp for safety.' Hiram moved to Hemsworth after the war and died in 1968.

January to July 1944

By the end of 1943 the councils had begun to compulsorily purchase houses for the rehousing of the townspeople.

In the Second World War, Barnsley boys from the York and Lancaster Regiment distinguished themselves on all fronts. Private E. Taylor described his adventures during the Battle of Minturno. Initial attempts to breach the western end of the line were unsuccessful and it was not until 17 January 1944 that the Garigliano River was crossed, and Minturno taken two days later. Seven o'clock on Thursday, 20 January 1944, was zero hour for a battalion of York and Lancasters in Italy and the following three days fighting formed one of the finest actions by the Y&L. Events were happening fast for the Barnsley private, but he recalled how one of many German machine-gun crews got to within yards but no nearer:

We were in a German slit trench. It was a colossal affair twenty feet deep. Those boys liked their safety. It was so deep that we couldn't see out of it, so we crawled out of it and over the top with our Bren guns, only to be fired at by a tank three hundred yards away. Just then we saw a German crew, four men with a gun coming up the slope with intentions of going all the way. We opened with our Brens and the four of them went to the ground writhing.

When the company got the order to withdraw we must have missed hearing it. There were six of us and although we looked left, right and behind, we could not see anyone. We knew Jerry was in front, there was no need to look there, but when we went back to the big trench we half expected to find him in it.

However, it was empty and there we sat, with everyone else gone away and three German battalions, what was left of them, on the other side of the hill. Just then we saw a German tank with infantry on it coming up the track to get around behind us. We decided it was time to go. We backed out of the trenches with Bren and Tommy guns pointing in their direction.

An estimate of German dead killed by the Y&L is difficult, but word came from another battalion which retook the feature that the slopes were covered with German dead.

Young British men were conscripted to work in the coal mines between December 1943 and March 1948. They were chosen by lot by their registration numbers. Nearly 48,000 Bevin Boys performed vital and dangerous work in coal mines, a largely unrecognised service. Many of them were not released from service for over two years after the Second World War ended. Some of the borough's first Bevin Boys were billeted in Wombwell and Dodworth when the billeting officer, Mr C. Knowles, received a request for rooms and reminded the council that these lads were many miles from home doing dangerous work and needed support wherever possible. It was explained that the young men would be at a training centre for one month, after which they would be drafted into the Old and New Carlton collieries and Monk Bretton colliery. Opinion was divided: most gave the Bevin boys a warm welcome, but some resented young men being drafted in who had never worked in a pit before. Those who knew

In response to a government appeal, some British schoolboys volunteered for coalmines. These are just starting training at Markham Main.

what life in the pits was like preferred the prospect of going to war than working in the mine. Winston Churchill said, on 22 April 1943, 'One will say: "I was a fighter pilot"; another will say: "I was in the Submarine Service"; another "I marched with the Eighth Army"; a fourth will say "None of you could have lived without the convoys and the Merchant seamen"; and you, in your turn, will say, with equal pride and with equal right, "We cut the coal".' Houses were in short supply for the Bevin Boys despite appeals from the councils. It was

Bevin Boys at Broadway Miners' Hostel take advantage of the snooker and table tennis facilities, then a hearty meal before work.

Bevin Boys laying the concrete pitch for a game of cricket. Some of these lads were skilled in their trained professions before the war.

decided to build two camps, one of which was on grassland in Broadway, off Dodworth Road. Forty-eight electrified Nissen huts were built by a Sheffield company. Each would house twelve miners – a population of 576. There was to be a dining hall 120 by 24 feet, a games room, a reading and a quiet room, a bathroom, shower blocks, a kitchen, a sick bay, a tea bar and accommodation for the admin staff. The manageress was Mrs Johnson. The theatre was one of their proudest achievements – the stage and its surroundings were built by the residents, and curtains were hung for the stage which was lit up by flood lights and arcs. Sports in the games room consisted of snooker, billiards, table tennis, darts, cards, dominoes and at the side was a gym with boxing facilities. The boys paid twenty-five shillings a week which included breakfast and the main meal. A smaller camp was built at the Carlton Hill site just off New Lane.

The story of the Bevin Boys wasn't always positive. Basil E. Southgate (18) who was lodging with a family in Darfield, decided to repay his hosts by stealing a bike, diamond rings and cash. Basil, a mining trainee, was sent to Great Houghton colliery and settled with the Lancasters, a family in the Darfield area who by all accounts helped him settle into the town. After Basil absconded he was eventually arrested in Norwich then found guilty of 'ripping off' the Lancasters.

Overseas, five Barnsley lads had reason to be proud after the historic all-day chase of the German capital ship *Scharnhorst* and her eventual demise at the Battle of the North Cape on 26 December 1943. At 16.17 the *Duke of York* made radar contact with *Scharnhorst*; thirty minutes later, *Belfast* illuminated the

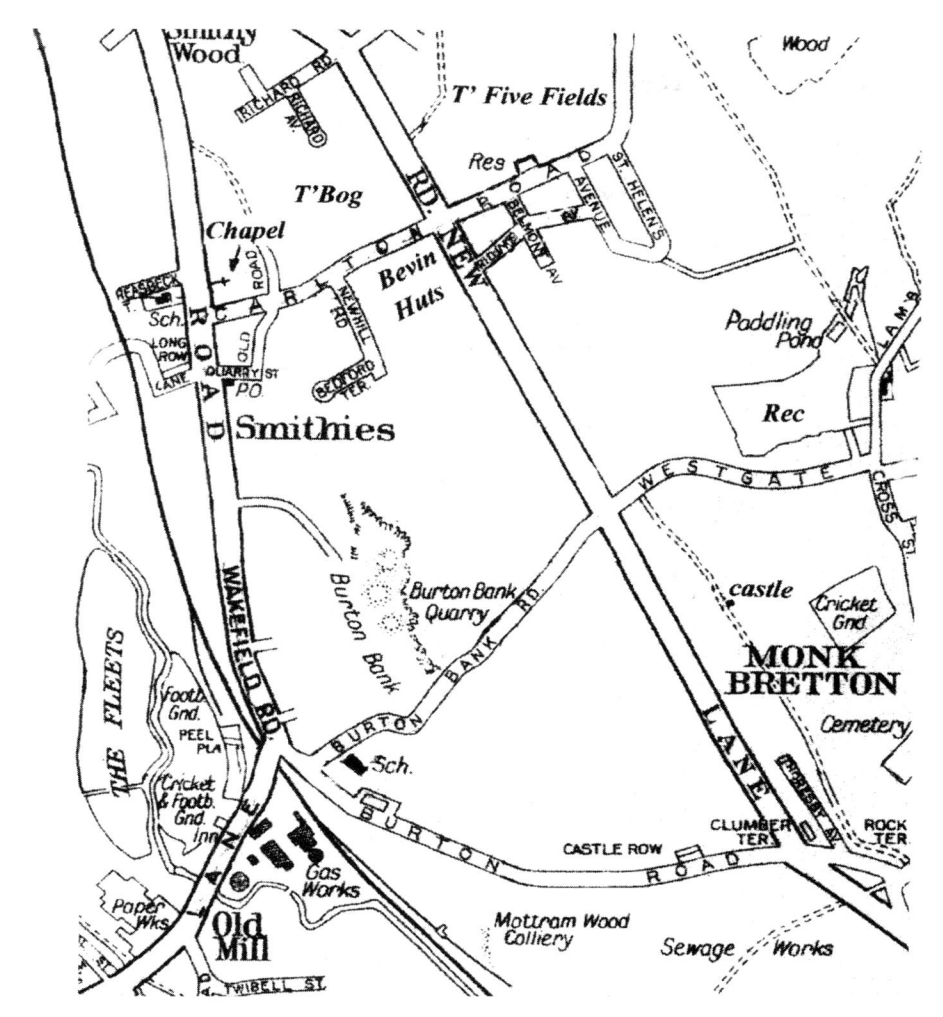

Map of Smithies showing the location of the Bevin Huts just off New Lane (now Rotherham Road). (courtesy of Memories of Barnsley)

German battleship with star shells. At 16.50 *Duke of York* opened fire at a range of 12,000 yards; *Scharnhorst* returned the fire. Five minutes after opening fire, one of *Duke of York*'s 14 inch shells struck *Scharnhorst* abreast of her forward gun turret. The shell jammed the turret's training gears, putting it out of action. Shell splinters started a fire in the ammunition magazine, which forced the Germans to flood both forward magazines to prevent an explosion.

Of the ships complement of 1,500, six were local men: Able Seaman Albert Wade (46) of 5 Regent Crescent, New Lodge; Blacksmith Eric Hepworth (22)

HMS Duke of York *in March 1942 escorting Convoy PQ 12.* (wiki commons)

of 44 Lambert Road, Kendray; Leading Stoker Horace Fearnley (49) of Cope Street; William Rock of The Square, Raley Street; Jack Crossland, formerly of 6 School Street, Darton; and Petty Officer Charles Francis Shaw of 86 Churchill Terrace, Royston.

William Rock described the action as a 'real Christmas box'. A member of the gun crew, he relates how the battle had started after they had safely escorted a convoy to Russia. 'We were told that the Scharnhorst was out and all the boys were on their toes. At 16:30 hours the order came to stand by for action and later, load. Then the fun started… We were told that the German ship was on fire and that the Duke had slowed her down so that our smaller boats could get in and finish her off.'

'The Barnsley Chop' was a Spitfire bought with the amalgamated contributions of the Barnsley Spitfire Fund and the Barrow Barnsley Main Colliery Spitfire Fund. Mk.IXc MH819 was named after the pre-war butcher's speciality. Taken on charge at No.33 MU Lyneham on 22 July 1943, the aircraft went to No.405 Aircraft Repair Unit at Heston on 14 August before being issued out to No.19 Squadron at Kingsnorth on 28 August. Most of its career was spent escorting bombers on their attacks in northern France and Belgium. It was reported that during one of these raids the Chop was attacked by F.W. 190s who made a hasty retreat. On another occasion, while over the coke ovens, the Chop was again attacked by F.W. 190s

The Barnsley Chop, Spitfire Mk. IXc MH819 on parade. It entered service in July 1943, eventually joining the Royal Hellenic Air Force in 1948.

which were about 20 feet below. This magnificent warbird survived the war and was transferred to the Greek Royal Hellenic Air Force from 20 April 1948.

Elsecar pit canteen welcomed King George VI and his wife Elizabeth on 9 February when they had lunch with miners at Elsecar Main Colliery. 'I must say,' remarked the Queen to a miner after lunching on roast beef and lamb, 'we haven't had a better meal for a long time.' Mrs Crossley said that this was a typical meal for a miner for a shilling. The seventy miners who joined the King and Queen at lunch were chosen by ballot, some having just come up the shaft from the day shift. On the King's right sat the checkweighman at the colliery, Mr A. E. Wilkinson, with Lloyd George and general manager Mr H. Danby making up the top table. Mr Wilkinson said afterwards, 'I felt very much at home with the King. He is a sociable man and broadminded.' The royal party visited a Darton school, then the Town Hall at Barnsley, hastily arranged by Gilfillan.

Over the skies of Europe, Barnsley pilots were distinguishing themselves. Pilot Officer 'Hank' Smith, diving through cloud, drizzle and fierce anti-aircraft fire to investigate a German airfield near the huge port of Wilhelmshaven. The field was free of airplanes but it was littered with ammunition. After a few bursts of the Mustang's cannon the boxes exploded violently. Hank, from Mapplewell, said, 'It must have been a dump, either petrol or explosive. Some pilots shot up two goods trains, causing considerable damage.'

At the sixth hour on the sixth day of the sixth month of 1944, men from Barnsley who had witnessed the great retreat at Dunkirk were back! It was reported that the first Allied soldier to land on D-Day was Bob Midwood of Mount Vernon Drive. Readers may remember Midwood Sports on Shambles

172   BARNSLEY AT WAR 1939–45

Above: Lieutenant Bob Midwood briefs his men before Operation Overlord.

Below left: Marjorie Midwood, wife of Fred who served as a FANY.

Below right: Ronald Tatchell who lived at Park Avenue, Penistone.

Street that Bob founded. Bob was a lieutenant with the Parachute Regiment and Operation Deadstick was the codename for an airborne operation by the British army that took place on 6 June 1944 as part of the Normandy landings. The mission's objective was to capture intact two road bridges in Normandy, across the River Orne and the Caen Canal, which provided the only exits eastwards for British forces from their landing on Sword Beach. Intelligence reports said both bridges were heavily defended and wired for demolition. Once captured, the bridges had to be held against any counter-attack until the assault force was relieved by commandos and infantry advancing from the British landing zone. Mirfield born, Bob Midwood served before the war as a bombardier in the Royal Artillery in India joined the police in Scarborough when he left the army in 1936.

Hundreds of Barnsley men, including Ronald Tatchell who lived at Park Avenue, Penistone, were able to land safely, in part due to the bravery of soldiers like Bob Midwood. Ronald joined in a sniper hunt in a wood in Normandy; their bag that day was sixty prisoners, three guns and the capture of an enemy strongpoint. The hunt took place on the 50th Northumbrian Division front, starting from a copse in which some gunners and Royal Engineers were waiting to move forward. Odd rounds from a wood 200 yards across the field kept flying over the heads of the British in waiting. Impatiently, armed with stens and rifles, they advanced to a copse to find the source of the fire but found nothing and went back for their flamethrower. The appearance of the flamethrower was too much for the dejected Germans, mostly boys and older men. 'Despite their strong positions, the Germans seemed glad to surrender,' said Ronald. Inside the wood they also found an 88mm and three 75mm guns (one of which had been destroyed) well dug in and camouflaged. Ronald, who was in the REME, died in 1991.

In another of these copses Lieutenant Arthur Douglas Hatfield met his end on D-Day + 11. Arthur lived at 15 Pollitt Street with his wife Margaret. In civilian life he was assistant to the Borough Engineer and carried this profession into the army when he signed up for the Royal Engineers in November 1940. Arthur was in a forward position when a sniper's bullet took him out, killing him instantly. He was buried at Bayeux War Cemetery.

Arthur Hatfield was in a forward position on D-Day at the time of his death when a sniper's bullet took him out, killing him instantly.

After being labelled a shirker for missing shifts, Royal Butterwood, who I mentioned earlier, finally revealed his true colours. Royal joined the York and Lancs in July 1943 but was transferred to the elite Paratroop Regiment four months later. Royal became cut off in France when his company was in action. After making several efforts to get back to his lines in between small pockets of Germans, he decided to lie 'doggo' in a wood, covering himself with moss until he got a chance to escape. During the night he said he was more or less surrounded by German soldiers. He could not sleep (no surprise) which was just as well because when a ten-man German patrol walked over him, even treading on his feet, he had to lie perfectly still. He lay in the wood for thirty-two hours before he was finally able to get away and return to his unit. Royal was married to Lillian and died in 1996 at the age of 78.

Nellie Marshall of Hough Lane, who graduated from St Andrew's Hospital in London, served the injured soldiers on the Normandy beaches in glorious summer weather. She was attached to the general hospital of the QAIMNS and saw first-hand the horror of the Allied attempt to win back Europe from Hitler. New shipments of wounded men would arrive from the front line hourly, each needing careful attention.

D-Day provided the local press with exploits of supreme bravery. It was also a time of remarkable coincidences. Driver Frank Wooffindin of Town Gate, Mapplewell, attached to the Field Ambulance, recalls this story. While going across to France in the first landing craft, he bumped into someone he knew, Clifford Mellor of Bence Lane, Darton. This they both thought was a special coincidence because they had already met in France and Italy. But another surprise awaited them as an LT craft pulled alongside and Frank recognised Richard Wilby of Paddock Road, Staincross. Needless to say, they greeted each other joyously.

Frank's younger brother Jack who was serving in the RAF in India had a similar experience. Upon going to a picture house in India, he was shown to his seat and sitting next to him was Sergeant Taylor of Staincross Common. Both had been members of the Staincross St John's Choir.

As hundreds of Barnsley men were scattered over Normandy in various roles, high above protecting them were the men of the RAF, many of whom came from the town. No. 409 Nighthawk Squadron flew the 'wooden wonder' – Mosquitos – over the Normandy beachhead in June: they scored eleven victories during this month. One of these kills was made by Flying Officer Alan Neison, and his observer Flying Officer Pat Smith who lived at Queens Drive, Barnsley, when they sent a Dornier 217 crashing in flames. Before blasting the Dornier, MacPhail had chased a Junkers 88 night-fighter but lost him in a cloud. Later, while circling to confirm the kill of the Dornier, the same Junkers picked up the Mosquito and started a high-speed dogfight. MacPhail weaved and dived his aircraft using all the evasive tricks in the book, but the Junkers stayed on until the Mosquito went into a vertical climb and peeled off at the top of it into a 400 mph dive which shook off the Hun. During the evasive action Pat was thrown against the cockpit cover jamming his face tightly against the windshield and then pitched back into his seat. Pat was also credited with bringing down two V-1 rockets.

In Worsbrough a huge crowd turned out for the visit of her Royal Highness the Princess Royal, Mary. At the outbreak of the war, the Princess Royal became chief controller and later controller commandant of the Auxiliary Territorial Service (later to become the Women's Royal Army Corps). In that capacity she travelled Britain visiting its units, its wartime canteens and its other welfare organisations. At Worsbrough she inspected the Worsbrough and District Nursing and Cadet Divisions at the Ambulance Hall, Worsbrough Bridge. Most of these women and the WVS would have attended to the sixty casualties from Normandy that arrived in Barnsley to be cared for at Beckett Hospital and St Helens Hospital, Pogmoor.

In Penistone a 'coloured' soldier, John T. Adam, was assaulted by Victor Kynaston who worked on the fairground. One evening at 10.10 pm John and a friend visited the Old Crown Inn on Market Street. In the pub was Kynaston and several other fairground attendants. They began making insulting remarks then the wife of Hugh McDonald the licensee ordered them to leave. A few minutes later when John was leaving the pub the three fairground men barred his path. Armed with a razor and a knife the men threw John to the floor, kicking and punching him. John's unit was so incensed with the attack, they banded together to seek justice for their friend. It was only thanks to the intervention of the police that a nasty situation was averted. Kynaston was charged with assault and fined.

In June and July the next savings campaign, 'Salute the Soldier', started and finished as admirably as the Wings for Victory campaign the year before. Each borough reached their targets.

In June the Germans started sending flying bombs also known as 'doodlebugs' or V-1 rockets into London. The war had become quiet on the home front by this time, but after a month of these rockets the government decided to evacuate some of the children. On 8 and 9 July 1944 special trains headed north full of apprehensive children; 680 were to stay in Barnsley then 85 each to Wombwell, Hoyland, Worsbrough, Cudworth and Darton. A fleet of twelve buses were waiting to take them to their destinations, the children to be billeted in Barnsley

Above: GIs stationed at Scout Dyke would have been familiar with this view of Penistone.

Below: Penistone Home Guard. (courtesy of Chris Sharp)

being housed for the night at rest centres, Baths Hall and Ebeneezer Church school room, where willing helpers had provided hot meals for the children and the London Council helpers. There was a huge crowd waiting for the trains including the mayor and mayoress and other town dignitaries.

A week later another train load of evacuees arrived making the total 1,424 children. It was a fantastic achievement for the town of Barnsley and her neighbours, maintaining their reputation for open-hearted hospitality. By September, 2,135 children had been relocated in the Barnsley area.

Experience of the billeting of evacuees were many and varied. Some were disgusted at the lack of community spirit, but in general the evacuees were well received by householders. There were complaints and grumbles by some and in other places direct refusals to take in other people's children. This was the case with the last contingent that was short notice. Efforts were made by the council to avoid compulsory billeting, but 84 mothers with 228 children still needed a home when compulsory billeting was introduced. The first prosecution for those who disobeyed the order was held in court a week later. Adam Gilfillan later recalled that the situation was far from pleasant for him: 'A lot of people I prosecuted were my personal friends,' he said. On the Monday the Chief Billeting Officer was able to report, 'All clear', meaning the last of the children had been found accommodation. It is worth noting that many letters appeared in the *Chronicle* from grateful Londoners who had a wonderful experience in the town.

This story has been added to the BBC People's War website by CSV volunteer Kate Langdon on behalf of the author Marjorie Chadwick:

It was in 1942 and I was only about 7 years old. I was sent off to Barnsley in Yorkshire with the school - Spring Grove Junior School, Isleworth. We were allowed to take up to one doll or toy, our gas mask and a case or small suitcase. We were given a label with the name and address which was tied onto my coat.

When we arrived and got off the packed train, we went to a community centre and slept on mattresses; there were no beds or anything. The next morning people came to claim us. They took their pick depending if they liked the look of you, then took us to their homes. Places were allocated to us for school.

The family I stayed with were ok, it was like a Coronation Street style house, two-up, two-down, with the front door on the main street. They had two children of their own and their father was a miner. He would come home black after a day working in the mines. I was well treated and fed well.

We would have Yorkshire pudding and gravy for tea. One of the boys from my school, who was on the train with me on the way up, wasn't so lucky. The home he went to was bad. A lot of people only wanted to look after us for the money they would receive because of it. But the boy was transferred to the family I was staying with.

My parents were invited by the family looking after me, to come up and stay for a holiday to get away from the bombing in London. They came up for two weeks, which I thought was rather nice of the people there. The bombing was bad on the Great Western Road [now the A4] which was about half a mile away from where I lived. A lot of the factories were making ammunitions for the war there.

My father was on the ARP and also worked for the Water Board in London, so he was out most nights mending broken water mains. I remember I used to sleep in the cupboard under the stairs most nights for about two to three years. It was meant to be the safest place in the house. Many a time I was 'chased home' from school by a 'Doodlebug', which was like a rocket V1/V2 bomber. It didn't have a pilot or anything and it would suddenly just stop and drop out of the sky. It was scary at that age being followed by one of them.

A little-known local fact is that Air Marshal T.W. Elmhirst, who ran the operations room at RAF Uxbridge on D-Day, was a local man from Worsbrough. Thomas was born on 15 December 1895 to Reverend William Heaton Elmhirst (b. 1856) and Mary Knight, a landed gentry family of Yorkshire whose family seat was at Houndhill. He was the fourth of eight boys and had one youngest sister.

In September it was announced by Home Secretary Herbert Morrison that the blackout would be eased. For the people of Barnsley it meant that from 17 September 1944 they would be able to use their ordinary peace-time curtains again and street lighting would be permitted in certain conditions in time for the ending of British double summer time – electric for some and gas lamps for others. Fireguard and other civil duties were modified by 12 September and the Home Guard was to revert to a volunteer basis from 11 September. Road blocks on the borough's roads were removed in early October.

Barnsley born Air Vice-Marshal T.W. Elmhirst.

In some theatres of war, however, the fighting was as intense as ever. In the latter part of 1944 more Barnsley men were killed than at any other time of the war.

Maurice Booth of Worsbrough Dale joined the Royal Artillery in November 1940 and was posted to the Middle East in 1941. He fought at 'Hellfire' Pass then at the Battle of Bardia and then took part in the second push across the Libyan Desert to Benghazi under General Auchinleck. Driver Booth was at the siege of Tobruk, and following its surrender in June 1942 was taken prisoner. He was taken to a camp at Benghazi where he spent five weeks in terrible conditions. He was then taken to a camp in Italy and after three months moved to another. Camp conditions were again very poor, but Red Cross parcels 'saved his life'. Booth said they had a fairly decent Christmas in 1942, despite being billeted at a factory with 1,500 other prisoners. His daily ration was a small quantity of brown bread and a little soup, and for recreation he spent most of his time in a field. While in Italy he met two Barnsley lads: Jim Booth, and Stanley Crossland of Summer Lane who was on the staff of the *Chronicle*. In May 1943, Maurice volunteered to work on a farm in northern Italy and with that came improved conditions. He stayed there until the Italian capitulation when he decided to make his escape. With no skin on his feet after four days of weary tramping he made it to the Swiss border. Maurice said that the Swiss treated him very well. He skated, skied, was free to do almost as he wished, and he met another Barnsley escapee, Tommy Burton of Dodworth Road. After repatriation he learned that his mother had sent him 3,000 cigarettes, but while prisoner he only received about 200. Maurice's story was not unusual: plenty of Barnsley PoWs made escapes; some like Maurice had reached home, others had died trying.

Maurice Booth of Worsbrough Dale who escaped Italy finding safety in Switzerland. Maurice was one of many Barnsley men who made the 'great escape'.

The Home Guard made their bow from the public stage on 8 December 1944 in a 'stand down' involving 2,200 khaki clad figures from the youthful to the stereotypical 'dad's army'. On that bleak December morning, Barnsley watched proudly as the men, with splashes of rain on their faces, marched past the saluting base on Churchfields. Taking twenty-three minutes to pass, the four battalions swung arms to the music of the 72nd Battalion Home Guard band. All showed their appreciation to the men who had worked tirelessly down the pits or in glass works but had still found time to do their bit. They included the highly trained 'tank trappers' or No. 3 Tank Trapping Company, one of only three formed in the country and whose headquarters were in the Parish Room in Church Street. Stand-down dinners were hosted all over the town and surrounding boroughs, including one attended by Lord Harewood. The WVS was not stood down, which was accepted as a great compliment by its women.

January 1945

Goods that were unavailable during the war started appearing in the very cold January of 1945, such as French nougat and chocolate.

Barnsley boasted a code breaker, in the form of Cyril Uttley of Dunford Bridge. Cyril received the award of the Oaks Leaves and Certificate for Distinguished Service in Action. Cyril showed early potential as a cryptologist, regularly winning prize crosswords from the *Sheffield Independent*. The following was contributed by a relative of Cyril, John Abbott of London:

My mother was one of Cyril's cousins and they were the only ones who moved south and lived in London after the war. My mother was two years younger and lived in Midhopestones. Cyril lived in Carlecotes (Dunford). They both went to Penistone Grammar School. In his year Cyril was one of four very bright lads at maths and the headmaster (a Quaker) used to set them special exercises as a group (I think he and his wife having invited them to their house for Sunday tea). The other boys were Dick Stuchbury, Charlie Stuart and Alec Challis (father of John Challis of Only Fools and Horses *fame). On leaving school Cyril took the Civil Service exams and I was told came second in the whole of the country that year. He became a senior civil servant in London working at the Board of Trade and Ministry of Transport.*

On the outbreak of war Cyril joined the Royal Navy (not wanting any square bashing) and was trained at HMS Royal Arthur *naval base (i.e. Butlins Skegness). At the end of the first week they were allowed home for a weekend break except those who could not swim and had to stay behind and learn. Cyril could not swim but did not want to miss the weekend break – he went through his whole naval career not being able to swim and not letting on! During the war, Cyril served on HMS* Honeysuckle *as a coder and was one of very few (and possibly the only) person to serve on the ship from its commissioning until the end of the war (when it was run aground at Milford Haven). The corvette's role was escort to the Arctic convoys to*

Russia. During his service, Cyril certainly visited Archangel and Murmansk in Russia and Halifax, Nova Scotia and Iceland.

There is a book entitled Honeysuckle's War: The Story of a Corvette *by Ian Claxton, a copy of which is in the National Maritime Museum. There is a picture of Cyril in a group on the ship and a couple of references to Cyril in the text. Apparently, when* Honeysuckle *was commissioned there was no ship's clock and, appreciating the importance, Cyril was instrumental in seeking support and funds to get one. On* Honeysuckle's *decommissioning Cyril was presented with the clock. In a quirk of fate, Cyril, when working at the Board of Trade immediately after the war, was given the job of disposing of surplus ships, including* Honeysuckle *which was broken up for scrap at Grays Thurrock. I understand, although I never saw it, that he was given the ship's wheel.*

Cyril was married to Pat (whose father I understand was a former mayor of Willesden borough). They lived in the Acton/Ealing area for a time but moved out to the Buckingham/Hertfordshire borders and for many years lived in Chorleywood. In family visits in the 1950s I can recall Cyril having my brother and I in fits of laughter (I always enjoyed his dry sense of humour). Cyril and my father used to play chess (my father was a very good player, Cyril was excellent!).

During Cyril's time at the Ministry of Transport, Roy Mason, MP for Barnsley, was the minister and he must have appreciated that in Cyril there was someone in the London civil service that knew his area. When Roy Mason was appointed the fourth secretary of state for Northern Ireland in 1976, he invited Cyril to be his principal private secretary. Cyril however declined having been told that he and his family would have armed police protection – I suspect by that time of his life Cyril thought he had been in enough dangerous situations already!

On retirement, Cyril and Pat lived in Norfolk for a time then returned to the Amersham/Chesham area. Pat died in 1986 and Cyril used to occasionally visit my mother until her death in 1995. In later years, Cyril suffered from dementia, but I used to enjoy my conversations with him as he retained his memory of his wartime years.

From September 1939 to November 1944, there were 631 incidents caused by enemy air activity in the West Riding County area. In the Barnsley area most incidents, 70, were reported in the Penistone area and 8 in the Staincross areas. The longest alert was in Penistone on the 21 December 1940: nine and a half hours. A flying bomb was seen over the area in December 1944 on its way to Manchester.

Barnsley's compulsory fire guard services were stood down on 14 February 1945.

Football followers especially would have regretted the news that Sergeant Fred Fisher (34) was killed. Freddy played as an old-fashioned outside right for Barnsley, then for Chesterfield, then just before the war for Millwall. He served in the Police War Reserve before joining the RAF about eighteen months before his death during an operational flight in a Lancaster bomber.

All crew of Lancaster LM386 coded AS-V killed when it was lost on a mission to Stuttgart. Airborne at 21:25 from Kirmington, near Grimsby, the aircraft crashed 00:40 between Aubigny (Yonne) and Taingy, 8 km W from the town of Courson-les-Carrieres. It is probable that LM386 was shot down by Oblt. Herbert Schulte zur Surlage of 5/NJG4 from 4,000 metres over the St. Sauveur area. Shortly afterward zur Surlage and his crew had to bail out of their JU88 G-1, possibly because of fire from LM386.

Freddy lived at 5 Gate Crescent, Dodworth, with his wife and five children; the eldest was 14. The Fisher family were bombed out twice in the London Blitz, forcing them to move to the relative safety of Barnsley.

On 5 April the Empire Cinema opened its doors to fifty service men on leave who were given free tickets to enjoy the film *Together Again* starring Irene Dunne. A few days later the Alhambra entertained 100 children whose fathers were still PoWs. Interned prisoners had been arriving home at a steady rate as both the Allies and the Russians advanced through Germany. On 28 April 1945, Mrs Jubb, the organiser of the Barnsley Prisoner of War Association, informed the council that most of the European prisoners had been liberated and were, to their great relief, back in Barnsley.

Mrs N. Jubb, the woman who worked tirelessly for the Barnsley PoWs, receiving a token of appreciation from the former mayor, Alderman Walton.

'It is lovely to be back in Barnsley, it has happened to quickly I can hardly believe it,' said Frank Rhodes, a 25-year-old of Harvey Street, Barnsley, who got taken prisoner by the Italians in June 1942. Such sentiments were shared by hundreds of repatriated Barnsley and district men who all had their own stories to tell. Many had been held in foul camps, put up with the derision of their often merciless captors, endured forced marches, sometimes starved almost to death.

Tuesday, 8 May, was a public holiday celebrated to mark the formal acceptance by the Allies of Nazi Germany's unconditional surrender. Barnsley celebrated VE day with a short message by the mayor followed by cars with loud speakers touring the district announcing the cessation of hostilities. After a thunderous storm, Union Jacks popped up all over the streets splashing the town with red, white and blue. Many people glued themselves to their wireless sets anxious to be the first to hear the declaration of peace. The town swung into a festive mood with jubilation and thanksgiving, though with half a mind on the men still fighting elsewhere, and most of VE day streets were kept quiet by the rainy skies. Nevertheless, the pubs were doing a brisk trade

Monk Bretton Castle, scene of jubilation after the war.

and the crowd partied well into the night. When dusk came the decorated Town Hall rose majestically in a floodlit glow. Narrow Market Hill produced some mammoth Union Jacks, and at Island Corner the Co-op had bedecked their premises with colour. To look along Cheapside, Market Hill or Eldon Street was to see a vista of flags. On May Day Green revellers kept dancing, drinking and laughing until the early hours of the morning, music played by loud speaker from the Town Hall. Margaret Marsh of Penistone worked for the Ministry of Food; her vantage point was on top of the Town Hall tower. Bonfires were popular, most topped by the effigy of the Austrian dictator. It was not until 2.30 am, the air thick with the smoke of fireworks, that the crowd went home.

Wednesday was a holiday too. The weather was much brighter and Cudworth, Royston and Hoyland had outside tea parties. One of the largest parties was on Wilthorpe Green. Children were seated on tables sixty yards long. At Ardsley and Stairfoot the residents on the Kendray Estate took advantage of the sun to give the kids a memorable day. Darton was full of colour with flags and bunting spread across the streets. For some time, wood for bonfires had been collected by children and there were several in the village, those on Sackup Lane and West Darton being especially huge. A tea party for Oaks Terrace was held in the Darton School, junior yard. Ash Grove Cottages held one at the back of their houses. Children of Sackup Lane and of Beaumont Buildings and the Woodlands held teas in the Zion Methodist Schoolroom and afterwards went to a bonfire made by Mr Sharp of Oakley House. Wentworth Road was one of the best decorated streets in Darton area; one of the huge bonfires had an effigy of Hitler with the inscription, 'The Devil is Dead'. The grandest bonfire was at Hoyle Mill: over 10,000 people watched a 30-foot-high wood pile with a Hitler effigy on the top. For some the war wasn't over: many streets had the motto, 'don't forget the boys in Burma,' a reminder that hundreds of Barnsley men were still fighting and dying for their town and country.

Back to work the next day, attendance of most local pits was about 70 per cent but at one it was just thirty. I don't suppose anyone would begrudge them sleeping off their hangovers. A crowd of only 527 watched as the Reds got thrashed 4-2 by Huddersfield Town.

In Germany, Belsen concentration camp was liberated on 15 April 1945 by the British 11th Armoured Division. The soldiers discovered approximately 60,000 prisoners inside, most of them half-starved and seriously ill; and 13,000 corpses, including those of Anne and Margot Frank, lying around the camp unburied. Gunner Philip White, a Barnsley soldier, gave his story; extracts are from letters home he wrote to his father:

About a fortnight ago before we captured the area two S.S. officers with a white flag came through to our lines and informed our officers that in the path of our advance was a Concentration camp with 60,000 criminal and political prisoners, both men and women and few children.

The S.S. officers asked the British Army not to shell the area, as it was neutral, and said the British troops would be needed to keep an eye on the eight hundred Hungarian and two hundred German (Wehrmacht) Guards.

We set out for the camp as soon as our tanks had outflanked the neutral area. As we rode in our tanks the sight that struck me most was the poor wretches. We were told they had no food for six days, and they had practically no water.

The food store in the camp had been broken open by the mob and we were sent into the enclosure to get them out. But what chance had a handful of British troops with rifles against 60,000 mad, starving prisoners. As soon as we got them out of one side they would be in at the other.

As we were herding them out the older ones were too weak to stand against the mob and just dropped and hadn't the strength to stand back up. We would find them in a couple of hours, stone dead. They had no shoes and stockings and hardly any clothes at all. Some stank and were as black as the fire back. The people have been starved for so long that now when they are able to get their food, their stomachs will not stand it, and they continue to die as before.

Their dead bodies were all over the camp. You could tell some had been shot dead by the S.S. men, others had been beaten to death, but most had died from sheer exhaustion and hunger. A man or woman would lie down on the ground in the warm sun, after tea, and would not have the strength to rise when dusk came when it began to get cold. Next morning, we would find them dead.

There was a woman you could only call her a living corpse carrying what was left of her baby, who kept whining and tugging at our uniforms and pointing to her bundle. One of the lads eventually understood what she wanted, just a tin of milk for the baby, next day they had both died.

You may read of this place in the papers or see it in the films and if so I should be on. This place is called the Black Hole of Belsen.

Arriving home after four years, the Barnsley 'Terriers', unmistakable in their khaki uniforms, with bronzed faces and Australian bush hats, were seen about the town. Two years before the war the men of the 5th York and Lancaster Regiment were converted into heavy ack-ack batteries to form part of the Royal Artillery. The beginning of the war saw them manning gun stations around Sheffield and from September to December 1940 they went to London to serve in the Blitz. Recalled after the Thursday night blitz on Sheffield (12 December 1940), they arrived at dinner time on Sunday, firing that same night as the Germans attacked again. Then followed a spell at Derby and Nottingham and next to Bingley to get fitted out for going abroad. In September 1941 they sailed from Glasgow aboard the *Almanzora*, around the Cape, calling at Freetown, having three days ashore at Durban, a day at Aden, then onto Port Suez. Christmas was spent at Qassasin. February 2nd found them bound from Egypt on the *Eastern Prince* for Bombay, then to Barrackpore near Calcutta where they built gun sites. After the gun sites were organised, Indians took over. The next move was to Asansol in Bengal where they spent a year defending the aerodrome and building gun sites. On to Dimapur, the 14th Army railhead, where more gun sites were built for Indian units to take over and a move was made into Northern Assam to a place called Panitola, a huge tea plantation. After defending an American airbase, they were drafted to Imphal. By April 1944 the Japanese had broken through from Burma, and the battery were beleaguered in the Siege of Imphal. They were cut off there until the end of May. After the war, the Commonwealth War Graves Commission set up cemeteries in Imphal and Kohima to commemorate the British and Indian soldiers who died during the battle. After the siege and the ensuing battle, the Terriers were engaged in road construction and then re-equipped for the big drive

Men of the Y&L 2nd Battalion rest while on patrol in the jungle of Burma wearing bush hats.

Four Royston schoolboys who met in Singapore close to the end of the war.

FOUR FORMER Royston schoolboys, who had not met for three years, had a surprise re-union in Singapore, recently. They were P.O. K. Vallender, R.N., son of Mr. and Mrs. B. Vallender, 19, East End-crescent, who formerly worked at the Ceag engineering works; and three L.A.C.'s in the R.A.F., H. Robinson, son of Mr. and Mrs. H. Robinson, 84, Cross-lane, was an employee of the Sheffield Gas Co.; D. Grant, son of Mr. and Mrs. T. Grant, formerly in the employ of the Y.T.C., and G. Neale, who formerly worked as a clerk with the Monckton Colliery Co.

through to Meiktila. The 4 Corps, of which they were part, were supposed to be fighting around Mandalay, but in utmost secrecy they won their way through the Genga valley, known as 'Death's Valley', with their division as the spearhead, and captured Meiktila. The Terriers played a valuable part in cutting the Mandalay–Rangoon Road thus stopping all supplies to Mandalay. They had crossed the Irrawaddy at Packakoo to Pagan. Having had a successful jungle campaign, the Terriers were due to return to England. Once relieved they flew out from Mengyan to Chittagong and from there to Gaya by road and river. Three days were spent at Gaya and then on to Deolali where they were fitted out for home. After three days stay there it was homeward bound on a troopship in Bombay. The only call was at Port Said where more troops were taken on board. They sailed through the Med and arrived at Glasgow at the end of June 1945.

A sergeant interviewed said, 'there had been a real spirit of comradeship among the Terriers. The Japs were tough if not clean fighters, but their worst enemy was climate and tropical diseases.' The Japanese suffered heavily during the campaign from malaria, cholera, and dysentery and some starved. The British had been given Mepacrine once a day which kept their malaria rate low. The highest temperature was 137 degrees in the shade, but the Australian type bush hats were a good protection.

The town was preparing for the first general election since 1935 and by the end of July the results were in. In Barnsley Frank Collindridge was re-elected for Labour.

Barnsley and other councils in the district were busy preparing new housing sites across the district. Land was bought in Penistone, Blackheath and Grange Farm at Athersley, New Lodge, Newtown Estate Cudworth and Kendray. Use of German PoW labour was proposed; Germans were already at work in Darton dredging the Dearne. Barnsley was one of the towns where the first post-war brick houses were built.

Victory in Japan day was, for Britain, 15 August 1945. VJ day was celebrated with the same enthusiasm as VE day in Barnsley and the districts.

During early September, even though the war had officially ended, Barnsley received 194 Dutch children and 33 adults to stay in a camp near the town. The incongruous children were visiting the town under recuperation plans of the Dutch government. Nearly all the children were described as 'poorly shod' as they arrived at the Courthouse Station where double decker buses transported them to the Bevin Boy camp on Carlton Road. Some had only eaten tulip bulbs and sugar beet for weeks. The billeting officer, Mr Anderson, made good on his promise to get the children settled safely.

Poems were sent back home by the dozen during the war. Here is one I would like to end my book with. It was written by Ordinary Seaman J. Johnson of Worsbrough Dale, composed while in a Naval hospital bed:

A Sailor thinks...
When at my door I used to stand
Summer evenings, peaceful and still,
I realised the wonder of nature's hand,
As I gazed at Dovecliffe and Blacker Hill,
Now I stand behind my Naval gun,
Ready for the cursed, brainless Hun
When we meet him the lads go mad,

These Dutch kids stayed at Smithies in the Bevin Huts. The headline to this image was 'Starving Dutch kids arrive in Barnsley.'

The first Dutch children who were cared for in Barnsley. They stayed at the Bevin Huts in Smithies.

And soon he is saying, 'Mercy, Kamarad.'
I've seen a lot since I left the Dale,
Now, like all sailors I can tell a tale.
You know what they say about the Navy,
Boys of Bulldog breed, that's true,
Now I will end my yarn, me hearties,
And say cheerio with a heart that's true,
So, when you are having your Christmas parties
I'll be thinking of Barnsley, the Dale and you.

Repercussions of the war can still be felt in Barnsley today. Men, women and children died for a part of England they loved, a piece of land they called home, a town called Barnsley.

For further information on those who died from Barnsley in conflicts including WW2 see www.barnsleywarmemorials.org.uk

Endnotes

1 *The Barnsley Independent*, Saturday, 17 October, 1925.
2 Elliott, B., *The Making of Barnsley*. Wharncliffe Books, 2004.
3 E.C. Ramsbottom, *Journal of the Royal Statistical Society*. Vol. 102, No. 2 (1939), pp. 289-91.
4 *The Barnsley Chronicle*, 10 December, 1938.
5 *Ibid.*
6 Orwell, George, *The Road to Wigan Pier.*
7 shirazsocialist.wordpress.com
8 Information on National Statistics.
9 Elliott, *Barnsley*, 2004.
10 *The Barnsley Chronicle*, 8 December 1938.
11 *The Barnsley Chronicle*, 29 October 1938.
12 Elliott, B., *Aspects of Barnsley*, Part 5. Wharncliffe, 1998.
13 lbmhs.co.uk/her-creking-country - *The Death of a Duchess* by Wendy Middlemass.
14 Causes of, and Circumstances attending, the Explosions which occurred at Barnsley Main Colliery, Barnsley, Yorkshire, on the 16th and 17th February 1942-11 August 1942, Major The Rt. Hon. G. Lloyd George, M.P., Minister of Fuel and Power.
15 See ancientmonuments.uk/118071-heavy-anti-aircraft-gunsite-330m-south-east-of-lowfield-farm-dearne-south-ward.
16 *A Hard Fought Ship: the story of HMS Venomous* by R.J. Moore and J.A. Rodgaard. Holywell House, 2017.

Index

Italicised numbers refer to illustrations within the text. Street names are in Barnsley and the Metropolitan Borough unless otherwise stated.

148 (Barnsley and District) Squadron, 62
189th Anti-Aircraft Battery RA, 19, 22, 37, 50, *51*
1st Battalion Yorkshire and Lancaster Regiment, 21, 44
1st Cadet Battalion Y&L Regiment, *89*
31st (North Midland) Anti-Aircraft Brigade, 26
43rd (5th Duke of Wellington's Regiment) Anti-Aircraft Battalion RE, 26
49th West Riding Division, 56
50th Northumbrian Division, 173
64 (Fighter) Squadron of Church Fenton, 51
67 York and Lancaster Anti-Aircraft Regiment RA, 24, 56
6th Battalion Y&L, 60

ACE Cinema (Royston), 109
Adam, John T., 175
Adams, George, 114
Afford, Private Lewis John, 163
AFS (Auxiliary Fire Service), 85, 97, 113, 118, 121
Aldershot, 93
Alhambra Cinema, 47
Allanach, James Arthur, 116

Allott, Alderman Reverend D., 25, 130
Anderson, Mr A., 96
Angel Hotel (Bolton-Upon-Dearne), 146
ARP (Air Raid Precaution), 8–9, 11, 15, 17–21, 30, 32–8, 41–2, 46–50, 60, 65–6, 76, 78, 83, *86,* 106, 113, 127, 139
ATS (Auxiliary Territorial Service), 95, 103, 124, *125,* 145, 159
ATS Detachment, 2WR Company, 24

Baedeker Raids, 144, *145*
Bailey, Sub-Lieutenant Leslie, *125*
Ball, Dr, 21
Banham, Police Constable, 62
Barebones, 13
Barker, Captain Harry, 119
Barley, John, 65
Barnes, Albert, 38
Barnsley (Barrow) Main Colliery, 22, 66, *67,* 77, *86,* 139–40
Barnsley Booklovers Club, 48
Barnsley Central School, 104
Barnsley Chamber of Commerce, 9
Barnsley Channel Islands Society, 95
Barnsley Chop (Spitfire), 170–1
Barnsley Chronicle, 9
Barnsley Co-operative, *9*

Barnsley Drill Hall, *8,* 17, 19, 22–4, 52
Barnsley Football Club, 32, 41, 49, 73
Barnsley Grammar School, 48
Barnsley Old Hall, 11
Barnsley Prisoners of War Association, 156
Barnsley Society of the New Church, 121
Barnsley Technical College, 11, 99
Barnsley Town Hall, 11
Barnsley War Weapons Week, 116–18
Barraclough, Gunner William, 93–4
Barraclough's Foundry, 30
Barrowclough, B.S.M., 22
Bates, Harold, 115
Battle of Minturno, 165
Battle of the North Cape, 168
Battle of the River Plate, 82
Bayford, E.G., 47
Beardsall, Private Jack, 93
Beaumont, Anne, 146
Beckett Hospital, 64, 94, 175
Beckett, Nurse Mabel, 94
Beech Grove School, *36*
Beeson, W., 45
Belfast, HMS, 168–9
Bentham, Mr F., 106
Berry, Mr, 50
Bevin Boys, 159, 166–9
Bevin MP, Ernest, 140–1, 143
Binns, Arthur, 38
Birdwell Drill Hall, 56
Birdwell, 39
Birt, Sergeant Stanley Basil, 163
Bismarck, 123, 125, *126*
Black Bull Hotel, 64
Boot, Maurice, 179
Booth, Jim, 179

Boyd, Emma, 109
Boys and Girl Order 1941, 139
Bradford City, 41
Brammers hardware store, 39
Brent, William, AKA Forsythe, 16
Brewster, Private Edith (AKA Lady Palmer of Kirkbymoorside), 24–5
Bridge, David C., 62
Briggs, Mr A., 86
Britannia Street, 10
British Restaurants, 120, *122*
British Unionist Party, 81
Brocklebank, George 'Bert', 81
Brown, Ernest, 46
Bunkers Hill, 10
Bunting, Mrs A., 76
Burke, Martin, 129, *130*
Burton, Tommy, 179
Butler, Chief Constable G.H., 37
Butterfields department store, 10
Butterwood, Royal and Lillian, 140, 143, 174
Butterworth, John, 124

Cadel, Orderly Sergeant, 20
Carlton, 41
Carr, Dorothy (Dolly), 136, *137*
Carr, Julia, 65
Carter, Miss Mary, 76
Casey, Molly, 131
Cassells, Mayor, 46
Caveney, Private Nora, 159
Caves, Lance Bombardier John, 59
Chadwick, Marjorie, 177
Chamberlain, Neville, 8
Cheapside, 26, 46
Chivers, Chief Petty Officer, 123
Church of England Infant School, Birdwell, 39

INDEX

Church of England Infant School, Worsbrough Bridge, 39
Clayton, Tom, *19,* 26, 35, 38
Coe, Cordelia, 84
Coldstream Guards, 26, 91, 163
Collindridge, Frank, 30–1, 47, 188
Collins, Stanley, 52
Cook, Sergeant James, 116
Cooper Memorial Garden, 17
Cooper, Lance Bombardier Harry, 59
Cooper, Ronald, 163
Cooper, Trumpeter Fred, 59
Cooper's Art Gallery, *55*
Cornfield, Levi, 63
Courageous, HMS, 71, *72*
Court House Station, 60
Crossland, Jack, 170
Crossland, Stan, 113
Crossland, Stanley, 179
Cudworth Modern School, 82
Cudworth, 29, 39, 50, 56–7, 75
Cumberland, HMS, 82
Cundy Cross, *97*
Curtis, Alan, 29

Dainty, HMS, 81
Dalen, Jan van, 158
Danks, Decontamination Superintendent W.G., 38
Darfield Main Colliery, 46
Darfield Main Colliery, 95
Darfield, 39, 57, 76
Darton School, 171
Davies, Lawrence, 146
Defoe, Daniel, 33
Degnan, Tommy, 16, *17*
Delight, HMS, 81
Derbyshire, Sergeant Peter, 139
Dieppe Raid, 147

Dig for Victory, 100–102, 116
Digby, Lincolnshire, 25
Dodworth Church, 120
Dodworth, 46, 49, 76
Doncaster, 22, 24
Dook, Lance Corporal Tom, 119
Douglas, Isle of Man, 53, 60
Dransfield, C., *46*
Drill Hall, Birdwell, 38
Duchess, HMS, 81–2
Duffy, James, 63
Duke of York, HMS, 168–70
Dundas, Flying Officer John Charles, 100
Dundas, Hugh, 100
Dunkirk, 60, 91–4, 100

Eames, Private Mavis, 159
Ebeneezer Church, 177
Eder Dam, 158
Edmonds, Flight Sergeant Roland, 137
Elleker, Mr, 50
Elliot, Brian, 10
Ellis, Norman, 120
Elmhirst, Air Marshal T.W., 178
Elsecar Main Colliery, 38, 171
Elvin, Trevor, 157
Emergency Defence Act, 8
Empress Atlantis, 164
England, Mrs, 21
Erwin, Gunner T.E., 22
Erwin, Lance-Bombardier J., 22
Erwin, Lance-Bombardier J.A., 22
Evans, George, 98
Exley Private Luke, *163* - 164
Eyre, Maureen, 124

Fairclough, Dr, 99
Falcon Engineering Works, 36

Fearnley, Leading Stoker Horace, 170
Feasby, Bob, 16
Ferrington, Michael, 132
Ferrymore Colliery, 34
Fielding, Sergeant, 46
Firth, Freddie, 81
Fisher, Sergeant Fred, 182
Frost, Lieutenant Corporal Norman, 88

Gibraltar, 81
Gibson, Guy, 158
Gilfillan, Adam Eric, 11, 13, 18, 30, 32–3, 41, 76, *96*, 171
Gilfillan, Evelyn, 76
Gledhill, Walter, 140
Graf Spee, 82
Greasley, Roy and Raymond, 108
Green, Private Harry, 88
Greenock, 81
Grenfell, David (Dai), 123
Griffiths MP, Mr George, 33, 116
Griffiths, Philip Julian, 116
Grimethorpe Band, *9*, 57
Grimethorpe, 34, 57
Group I, Sector 3, Barnsley Civil Defence, *67*
Grove Street School, 99

H. Field and Son, 121
Haigh, Harold, 163
Halifax Town, 73
Hall, Joseph, 95
Hall, Lieutenant J., 22
Hallamshire Battalion, 60
Hallworth, John, 16
Hardcastle, Charles, 139
Hardware, Able Seaman Leslie Gordon, 160
Hardware, Cyril B., *149*

Harral, Benjamin, 22
Harrington, General Charles, 7
Harrison, Stoker Jack, *81,* 82
Hatfield, Lieutenant Arthur, 173
Hawcroft, Agnes, 104
Hawcroft, Bernard, 144
Hawcroft, Dorothy, 104
Hawcroft, Winifred, 131
Hawkins, Anne, 75
Hawthorne Crescent (Dodworth), 52
Hayhurst, Police Sergeant, 34
Hazzard, Jack, *134,* 135
Hecla, HMS, 148, *149*
Hemsworth, 33, 71, 165
Heppenstall, George Henry, 16, *17*
Heppenstall, Mr J.C., 86
Hepworth, Blacksmith Eric, 169
Hill, Able Seaman Gunner Ernest, 154–6
Hilly Fields (Wombwell), 37
Hirst, Albert, 10, 46, 72, 123
Hitchen, Gunner George William, 59
Hollingworth, Alexander 'Bruno', 135, *136*
Hollway, Frank, 50, *52*
Holmfirth, 26
Holt, Corporal Harold, 156, *157*
Home Guard, *8*, 88, 90, *91,* 97, 103, 118, 120, *121,* 123–4, 126–7, 144, 154, 156, 178–9
Honeysuckle, HMS, 180–1
Hood, HMS, 123, 125–6
Horbury, Harold, 16
Horn, Edith, 131
Horse and Jockey Hotel, 88
Horsfall, David Taylor and Albert, 158–9
Horton, John, 63
Howard, Connie, 101

INDEX

Howard, Seymour, 31
Hoyland Miners Hall, 57
Hoyland, Miss Elizabeth, *76*
Hoyle Mill, 42, 74
Huddersfield, 26
Huddlestone, Chief Detective Superintendent, 90
Hudson, Leading Stoker Jeffrey, 137, *138*
Hughes, Harry, 82
Hull, 121
Humphries, Mr, 50, 56

Ibbotson, Private Albert, 109
Iceland, 119–20
Irwin, Lance Bombardier Alf, 59
Ivimey, Mr H., 124

J. Lodge & Sons, 73
Jacksons furniture store, 14
Jefferson, Arthur, 57
Jehovah's Witnesses, 80
Jersey, 95
Johnson, Ordinary Seaman J., 188
Jones, Alderman Joseph, 48, 95
Jones, Alderman, 18
Jones, Joseph
Jubb, Mrs N., 182

Keel Inn, *97*
Kerr, Sister Julia, 151–3
Kexborough School, 144
Killingbeck, Harry, 74
Kirk Balk Senior School, 38
Kirkburton, 26
Knowles, Mr C., 96
Kynaston, Victor, 175

Lancaster JP, Mr Thos, 78
Lancaster, Alice Hilda, 77–8

Lancaster, Captain Bingley, 78
Lancaster, Janet, 146
Land Girl, 101–102, 157
Langdon, Kate, 177
Leeds United, 73
Lenton, Marion, Iris and Philip, 123
Leslie, Flight Mechanic Herbert, 144
Lightowler, Ed, 82
Locke Park, 56, 121, 123–4, 146
Longley, Elsie, 65
Low Laithes Farm, 102
Lowfield Farm, 146
Lundwood Military Hospital, 78
Lundwood Picture Palace, 57
Lundwood Smallpox Hospital, 126

Mackenzie, Major D.M.S., 20
Maisky, Ambassador Ivan, 143, *144*
Makeig-Jones, Captain William Totfield, 71
Maltas, Mr, 113
Manders, Bombardier, 59
Mapplewell, 13
Markham Main, 166
Marrison, Private Hiram, 164
Marsh, Margaret, 184
Marshall, Nellie, 174
Mason MP, Roy, 181
Mason, Mayor George, 80
Mason, Norman, 16
May Day Green, 65
McDonald, Hugh, 175
Measborough Dyke, 48, 131
Mellor, Clifford, 174
Mellor, James R., 47
Midwood, Lieutenant Bob, 171, *172*
Midwood, Marjorie, 172
Miller, Marine John, *147,* 148
Mills, Private Clifford, 84

Ministry of Labour Gazette, 11
Mirabelle Dancing Troupe, 106
Mirfield, 26
Mitchell, Garry, 64
Monk Bretton Castle, 183
Monk Bretton Home Guard, 78
Monk Bretton Station, 147
Morgan, Mayor Margaret, 17
Morley, Sergeant, 22
Mott, Ernest, 146–7

Neil, Colonel, 126, *127*
Neison, Flying Officer Alan, 174
Nelson, Colonel G.S., 22
Newsome, Marine George, 71
Norway, 87

O'Meara, James Joseph 'Orange', 99, 100
Old Cock Inn, 27, 29
Old Crown Inn (Penistone), 175
Old Keel Inn, 120–1
Old Windmill Hotel, 85
Oldham, Major G.H., 26
Operation Deadstick, 173
Operation Dynamo, 91
Operation Sea Lion, 97
Operation Source, 161
Orduna, SS, 120
Orwell, George, 13
Owen, Stoker Horace, 148
Oxley, Stoker William, 161

Palace Cinema (Royston), 140
Palfreman, Mike and John, 146
Paling, W., 47
Pallet, Joseph, 80
Parker, Shirley, 90
Parkin, Kath, 106–107

Penistone Drill Hall, 26, *28*
Penistone Grammar School, 180
Penistone, 26–7, 32, 34, 39
Pennines, 26
Pheasant Inn, 63
Pickering, Regimental Sergeant Major G.W., 53
Platts Common, 38, 57, 67
Pogmoor Refuse Works, 78
Pogmoor, *79*
Polyanthus, HMS, 160
Potts, Lewis, 80
Prince of Wales, HMS, 129

RAF Honington, 85
Raley School, 99
Raley, Alderman, 18
Ramshaw, Sergeant Pilot Jack, 84
Ratcliffe, Gunner Douglas, 139
Redfearns, 84
Redhill gang, 118–19
Regent, HMS, 137
Renshaw, Marine George, *71,* 147
Reykjavik, 120
Rhodes, Frank, 183
Richards, Councillor, 139
Richards, Councillor, J., 50
Rideal, Major J.G.E., 11, 13, 90, 103
Robinson, Mr F.G., 99
Robinson, Sergeant John, 163
Rock, William, 170
Rockley Woods, 24
Rollins, Joan, 124
Roper, Private William, 77
Rotherham Drill Hall, 24
Royal Army Ordnance Corps, 74
Royal Arthur, HMS, 180
Royal Horticultural Society, 116
Royal Hotel, 55, 124

INDEX

Royal Ordnance Corps TA, 55
Royal Tank Regiment, 119
Royston Benevolent Fund, 116
Royston Carnival Flower and
  Vegetable Show, 116
Royston Land Fertility Scheme, 116
Royston Royal British Legion
  Club, 116
Royston, 32, 50, 56
Rushworth, Frank, 64
Ruston, Gunner Percy, 148

Sargeant, Fred, *114*
Scarrott, Sergeant Wilfred, 110
Scharnhorst, 168–70
Scholey, William, 80
Schroeder, Albert, 80
Schuhart, Captain Lieutenant Otto, 71
Scout Dyke, 176
Sellers, Thomas, 104
Shaw, Joseph, 41
Shaw, Petty Officer Charles Francis, 170
Shaw, William, 109
Sheffield, 54, 60, 94, 110–11, *112,*
  113–14, 146, 185
Sheldon, Mary, 116
Shepherd, Mr J.R., 38
Sheringham, Norfolk, 59
Shield, Mr T., 39
Ship Inn, Worsbrough Bridge, 44
Shoesmith, E., 27, 29
Siege of Imphal, 186
Silkstone Fall Colliery, 73
Silkstone, 27
Simm, George Henry and Phyllis, 115
Sinnett, Corporal, 20
Skipton, 76
Slater, Sergeant E., 22

Smith, Flying Officer Pat, 174–5
Smith, Pilot Officer 'Hank', 171
South Kirby Colliery, 59
Southgate, Basil E., 168
Spanish Civil War, 16–17
Spring Grove Junior School, 177
St. Helens Hospital, Pogmoor, 175
St. Helens Hospital, 48
St. Luke's Church, 115
St. Luke's School, 121
St. Mary's Parish Church, 103
St. Marys Gate, 53
Steele, J.R., *21*
Steeples, John W., 146
Stephens, Guardsman Ronald, 91
Stewardson, Sister Olive, 151–3
Stores, Gunner R.V., 22
Strathallan, SS, 151–2
Sykes OBE MC TD JP, Colonel K., 26
Sykes, Corporal William, 99
Sykes, Ernest, 147
Symons, Captain H.A. Peter., 46, *69*

Tatchell, Ronald, 172
Taylor, Divisional Surgeon T.H., 20
Taylor, Private E., 165
Taylors Mill, 52
Thomas, Mr S., 50
Thompson, Emma, 132
Three Cranes Hotel, 47, 83, 99
Tipping, Mr J., 78
Tirpitz, 161–2
Tobruk, 115, 146, 179
Tomlin, Dr, 76
Townend, Edric Clifford and Edith, 147
Trueman, Mayor Samuel, 148
Trueman, Percy Coverdale, 64
Turner DFC, Captain S., 56
Tynwald, SS, 60

U-29, 71
U-238, 160
U-952, 160
Umbers, Squadron Leader E.H., 62
Umpleby, Eileen, 66
United Nations, 146
Unwin, George Cecil 'Grumpy', 109, *110*
Uttley, Cyril, 180

VAD nurses, *18,* 20–1, 31–3
Vernon Dunk Ltd., 121
Vickers, Gilbert, 136

Wade, Able Seaman Albert, 169
Wagstaff, John, 48
Wakefield Challenge Cup, 22
Wakefield County Hall, 26
Wakefield, Violet, 157
Wales, Colonel C.E., 53
Walker, Colonel James, 90
Walter Dunk & Sons, 62
Walton, First Class Stoker James, 129
Walton, Mayor James (Jim), 97, 124, 127, *128,* 129
Walton, Mayoress, *134*
Walton, Wilfred, 41
Wangerooge, 85
Ward, Stephen, 16
Watkins, Miss Gwen, 56
Watson, Henry, 46
Watson, Nancy, 131
Watson, Susan, 46
Webster, Harold, 59
Wellard, James, 151
Wellington Hotel, 157

Wentworth, 26
West Bank (Hoyland), 39
West Riding Council, 26
Wetherill, Flight Sergeant William, 163
Weybourne, Norfolk, 53, 57, 59
Wharncliffe Woodmoor, *17*
White, George, 83
White, Gunner Philip, 184
Wieck, Helmut, 100
Wilby, Richard, 174
Wildsmith, Clarence, 16
Wilhelmshaven, 85, 171
Williams, Chief Constable H.T., 85
Winter, Worsbrough Chief Air Raid Warden, 50
Wire Trellis Hotel, 65, 157
Wm. Johnson and Sons, 121
Wombwell Main Colliery, 115
Women's Voluntary Service (WVS), 76–7, 106, 121, 144, 175
Wood, Haslam, 42
Wood, Horace, 37
Wood, John Grantham, 163
Wood, Sir Kingsley, 42
Wood's Glassworks, 24, 42
Woodcock, Eileen, 124
Woodhall, Aircraftwoman 2nd Class Rieta, *150*
Wooffindin, Driver Frank, 174
Woolley Colliery, 140
Worsbrough Bridge National School, 81
Worsbrough reservoir, 22
Wright, Mayor Andrew, 21, 34–5,

Zeppelins, 34